Building Kitchen Cabinets
and Bathroom Vanities

Building Kitchen Cabinets
and Bathroom Vanities

STEVE CORY

The Taunton Press

The Taunton Press
Inspiration for hands-on living®

The Taunton Press, Inc., 63 South Main Street
PO Box 5506, Newtown, CT 06470-5506
e-mail: tp@taunton.com

Editor: Christina Glennon
Copy Editor: Candace B. Levy
Indexer: Jay Kreider
Cover design: Jean Marc Troadec
Interior design: Tinsley Morrison
Layout: Laura Lind Design
Illustrator: Mike Wanke, except where noted on p. 198
Photographer: Steve Cory and Diane Slavik, except where noted on p. 198
Cover photographer: Dan Stultz

The following names/manufacturers appearing in *Building Kitchen Cabinets and Bathroom Vanities* are trademarks: Automaxx™, Bench Klamp System™, Corian®, FastCap®, Formica®, Forstner®, Kreg®, Phillips®, Rev-A-Shelf®, SketchUp®, Space Balls®, Speed® Square, Titebond®, Vix®, Wite-Out®

Library of Congress Cataloging-in-Publication Data
Cory, Steve.
  Building kitchen cabinets and bathroom vanities / Steve Cory.
      pages cm
  Includes index.
  ISBN 978-1-62710-793-8
1. Kitchen cabinets. 2. Bathroom cabinets. I. Title.
  TT197.5.K57C675 2015
  684.1'6--dc23

                          2015019767

Printed in the United States of America
10 9 8 7 6 5 4 3 2 1

About Your Safety: Homebuilding is inherently dangerous. From accidents with power tools to falls from ladders, scaffolds, and roofs, builders risk serious injury and even death. We try to promote safe work habits. But what is safe for one person under certain circumstances may not be safe for you under different circumstances. So don't try anything you learn about here (or elsewhere) unless you're certain that it is safe for you. Please be careful.

Acknowledgments

The following individuals and businesses helped in the creation of this book:

Windy City Counter Tops (www.windycitycountertops.com), Chicago-area fabricators and installers of granite and other stone countertops.

Mike Fish of Vogon Construction (www.vogonconstruction.com), Chicago-area home remodeling and cabinetry.

Kokontis & Company Woodworking (www.kokontisandcompany.com), cabinetry, furniture design, and fine woodworking serving suburban Chicago.

Sommerfeld Tools (www.sommerfeldtools.com), suppliers of advanced woodworking tools for cabinetmakers.

Owl Hardwood Lumber Company (www.owlhardwood.com), suppliers of fine hardwoods.

Mike Anderson of Quality Solutions, fine woodworking for residential, commercial, and marine applications, in Olympia, Washington.

Kreg® Tools (www.kregtool.com), makers of joining, clamping, and fastening systems for professionals and do-it-yourselfers.

Rev-A-Shelf® (www.rev-a-shelf.com), makers of cabinet organizers and shelving.

Thanks to: Mike Fish, Mike Anderson, Danny Campana, Richard Andrews, Tom Kokontis, Dan Vejr, and Christina Glennon.

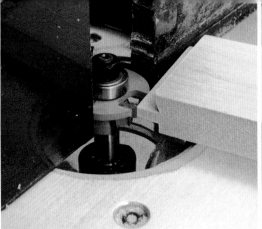

contents

introduction

UNLIKE MOST woodworking projects, kitchen cabinets are rarely built as single units. Instead, it usually makes sense to plan for a whole set, buy the materials, and custom-build a series of cabinets that neatly line up and fit the space requirements. While some of the work may be a bit factory-like, the custom-design aspect makes it more creative, interesting, and satisfying—letting you add variations wherever you need them in order to make the best use of your kitchen space.

Whether you are an experienced woodworker with a shop full of pro-level tools or a do-it-yourselfer with a few stationary tools in a garage or basement space, this book will enable you to build kitchen cabinets that will stay great looking and easy to use for decades.

If you are low on skills, time, or tools, you may choose to build only the cabinet cases and the drawer bodies yourself. You can then order doors and drawer faces from a company. If you're feeling

more ambitious, I'll show you how to build some simple doors and drawer faces, including slab and cottage style. And if you have the time, skills, and tools, I'll show you how to build more elaborate doors and drawer faces with details like raised panels and milled rails and stiles.

Why build yourself instead of buying ready-made cabinets? Here are some good reasons:

- Inexpensive ready-made cabinets are usually poorly made, often with particleboard cases that are inadequately stapled together. They typically have cheap hinges and weak drawer glides. Building yourself allows you to choose quality materials.

- Better-quality ready-made cabinets will cost a great deal more money. Depending on the materials you choose, you can often save quite a bit by building yourself.

- Ready-made units come only in standard sizes and usually require spacers—that is, vertical strips to fill in dead space between cabinets. When you build yourself, you can achieve a classier custom look with cabinets that fit like a glove, while also eliminating wasted space.

- Let's not forget the satisfaction that comes from building something yourself—not just the sense of accomplishment at the end but also the good feeling that comes from the process of designing and building a one-of-a-kind kitchen.

- The unique kitchen that you build can fit your family's needs to a tee. You can size cabinets, drawers, and shelves so your plates, glasses, pots and pans, and appliances fit neatly and comfortably.

How to Use This Book

Because there are so many styles of cabinets to choose from, you will no doubt end up picking and choosing your way through this book, to find the instructions that apply to you. I've arranged the book to make that process as smooth as possible.

PLAN, PLAN, PLAN

You may be the type of person who likes to start building, and then read instructions only when necessary. That approach often works for making individual pieces. But a kitchen generally includes dozens of cabinets and appliances that need to fit together perfectly. Any experienced kitchen remodeler can tell you a number of stories about costly mistakes due to rushing the design process. So before you go out and buy materials, sit back in your favorite chair and spend some quality time with this book. Good plans save time and money.

STYLE AND COST

First, choose your cabinet style or styles. (Cabinet cases are basic and boxy; it's the doors and drawer faces that set the tone.) This decision involves both aesthetic and practical considerations—that is, what looks good and what you can reasonably afford to build.

Once you've narrowed your style choices, check out chapter 8 and look for the sections that describe the building process for your style selections. Find out all the tools you will need (chapter 2) and make a realistic assessment of your skills. If building your chosen type of door seems daunting, perhaps choose another, simpler, style.

MATERIALS AND FINISH

Chapter 3 introduces most of the materials—sheet goods and hardwoods—available for building cabinets. Of course, you will want to take costs into account when choosing your materials.

Using information from chapter 1, make a drawing of your proposed kitchen. Use the info found at the beginnings of chapters 4 and 5 to calculate materials needed for the cabinet cases. Then figure the materials you will need for making the drawer bodies and shelves (chapter 7). Finally, calculate the materials for doors and drawer faces (chapter 8). Add it all up and choose a material you can afford.

Finally, consider whether you want to apply a simple finish coat or a stain plus finish or perhaps you'll choose to paint the cabinets.

MIX IT UP

As you peruse style options for your cabinet doors and drawers, consider combining different styles or colors to make the overall design more interesting. For instance, if you like the Mission style, you might consider complementing that basic choice with sections of cabinets that vary the design or color. One easy way to do this is to swap out wood panels for glass in one section of the kitchen (there are a number of glass options, including beaded and frosted). Or you can use the slab style on drawer faces. To vary the color, consider using a contrasting stain or painting cabinets in one area of the kitchen, perhaps along a short wall or an island. Think of the design process as painting with a large paintbrush: A few graceful strokes break up the monotony of all the cabinets in the same color and design. You can tie the design together with details like cove molding at the top of the cabinets or complementary handles. Design software can help you visualize the possibilities.

1

design

IF YOU'RE going to invest the effort and money into building your own kitchen cabinets, you'll want to be sure to get just the look and design you want. In addition to choosing a style that pleases you and your family, be sure to provide spaces tailored for your family's needs, such as shelving and cabinet space for dinnerware, glassware, and cookware as well as ample storage to keep small appliances tucked away yet within easy reach. When you build yourself, you can design drawers, cabinet openings, and shelves that are just the right depth, width, and height for your favorite kitchen items.

Kitchen design involves more than the cabinets, though. Plan meticulously to include appliances—notably, a refrigerator, range or oven and cooktop, dishwasher, and vent fan. Also plan for lighting and electrical outlets, including those on the wall between the countertop and the wall cabinets. It's common to measure for countertops after the cabinets are installed, but you may want to choose them both ahead of time.

Don't forget to plan for special amenities. You may, for instance, want a lazy susan for a corner cabinet, a pull-out garbage bin, or a shelf organizer of a certain type. Be sure to build cabinets that will successfully house the features you want.

Kitchen Planning

Even if you think you already know exactly what you want, don't hesitate to consider new kitchen design ideas. Visit kitchen design showrooms and home improvement stores. Stroll electronically through sites like Houzz (houzz.com), where you can quickly look at hundreds of kitchens. Leaf through kitchen-design and home-improvement magazines.

THE WORK TRIANGLE, UPDATED

A classic kitchen design principle states that the cooking surface, the sink, and the refrigerator should be arranged at the ends of an imaginary triangle, so that all three features are within easy reach of each other—but not too close together. Added together, the three sides of the triangle should total no more than 26 ft. and each leg of the triangle should be between 4 ft. and 9 ft. long. The area inside the triangle should, ideally, not overlap with a major traffic area; people should be able to travel through the kitchen via another route.

The triangle is definitely a good idea. However, things often get complicated. For example, most kitchens today have a dishwasher (which often gets used more than the sink) and a microwave oven (which may get used dozens of times per day). Also, a classic triangle is easy to achieve if your kitchen is U-shaped or if it has an island. But many kitchen spaces will not allow to you to form a perfect triangle. So use the triangle as a starting point but then think things through:

- Are you designing primarily for one cook or will there often be two or more cooks? If the latter, make sure each has his or her own work

This kitchen incorporates the refrigerator, sink, microwave, dishwasher, and range into a space that is fairly compact without feeling too tight.

CLASSIC KITCHEN TRIANGLE

The basic work triangle is a useful way to start a design.

Sink

Dishwasher below

Kitchen work triangle

Range/cooktop

Refrigerator

In a long, narrow kitchen with a door at the end, a triangle is simply not possible. Still, the refrigerator, dishwasher, sink, range, and microwave are positioned so that the longest distance (between the fridge and the microwave) is not too much of a schlep.

In a large kitchen, a large island opposite the main counter provides a number of conveniently placed surfaces and appliances for cooking, washing, and preparing.

tip

Many people prefer to place the sink at a window, because it makes dishwashing a bit more pleasant and, well, it's just traditional. However, there are other considerations: If you have a dishwasher, you will probably spend more time working on a countertop or a cooktop than at the sink. If your current plumbing is far from the window, moving it could be expensive. And if a sink at the window causes you to have your back to the rest of the house, you may prefer a different location.

surface as well as access to the refrigerator and cooktop without bumping into the other cooks too often.

- If kids are around, they will likely want to get at the refrigerator and the microwave several times a day. You may want to position those appliances so snackers will not interfere with the cook.

- If traffic often flows through the kitchen—say, to a much-used back door—try to provide a pathway that doesn't run through the food-prep area.

- Avoid bottlenecks whenever possible. For instance, if there is a single 3-ft.-wide doorway leading from the dining room to the kitchen, it may be worth the effort and expense to open the wall up and provide wider access.

- Will the kitchen be used for other purposes besides meal prep? For instance, will it be a spot for eating informal meals, possibly in a breakfast nook or at a cantilevered counter with stools? The kitchen may also function as a place for hanging coats and taking off boots if there isn't

Don't be afraid to incorporate non-kitchen elements into a kitchen. Here a coat rack is convenient to the back door.

a separate mudroom. And many people appreciate having a small office desk in the kitchen.

- If you do not have a separate pantry, you may want to section off part of the kitchen with floor-to-ceiling cabinets to create a pantry area.

Details, Details

If you hang around kitchen remodelers long enough, you're bound to hear a story like this: Someone goes to great expense and effort to build and install a dozen or more kitchen cabinets, only to discover—sometimes, at the very end of the job, perhaps when the range is wheeled into place—

that something doesn't fit quite right, so that a door or drawer will not open fully or may not open at all. As a result, several cabinets need to be removed and replaced. With careful planning you can avoid this discouraging scenario.

Measure the room carefully, down to an eighth of an inch. Walls may be out of plumb, so measure between two walls at several heights, and use the shortest measurement.

You can use a software program to design your kitchen or you can make a simple plan view drawing, as shown in "Plan View" on p. 9. You can easily and clearly include both wall cabinets and base cabinets in the same drawing because wall cabinets are half the depth of base cabinets.

KITCHEN DESIGN SOFTWARE

You can buy a three-dimensional kitchen design program, also called a CAD (computer-aided design) program, for kitchens for $100 or less. Several software companies make them. Visit online forums for discussions of various programs.

Many builders have found that SketchUp® meets all their needs; it has become the lingua franca of the construction world. It allows you to create your own cabinet designs or choose from a vast library of ready-designed cabinets from its "3D warehouse." The free version of SketchUp meets most people's needs, but you can also purchase an enhanced version for more features.

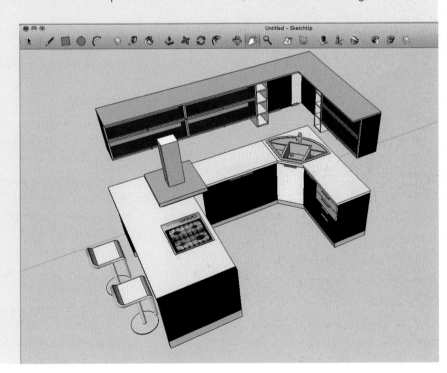

Before you draw or work with software, make sure you know the exact required openings for all your appliances, such as for the refrigerator, range, and dishwasher as well as for the sink. For example, a refrigerator is typically 32 in. or 36 in. wide and a modest range is usually 30 in. wide. You will probably build a base cabinet for the sink; make sure the cabinet is large enough.

Pay special attention to door clearances: Make sure you will be able to open the refrigerator, oven, and dishwasher easily as well as the doors to the adjoining cabinets. Where cabinets meet side walls, it's usually best to allow for a 1½-in. space, which can be filled with a spacer piece, so that doors can open fully. If you have an island, allow at least 42 in. of space between it and facing cabinets and appliances; 48 in. is better if you expect multiple cooks.

Also make an elevation view (see "Elevation View" on the facing page) or rotate your CAD drawing so you can look at the cabinets from the side. The gaps between doors will vary depending on the style you choose.

BASIC DIMENSIONS

In most cases, a wall cabinet is about 12 in. deep. (The wall cabinets I show later in the book, for example, have bodies that are 11½ in. deep and overlaid doors that are ¾ in. thick, for a total depth of 12¼ in.) You can make your wall cabinets 30 in. tall, which will leave a space on top for storage or a soffit. Or you can make them 42 in. or taller, so they reach the ceiling.

At the bottom of the base cabinet there is a toekick, typically 3 in. to 4 in. high and deep, which makes it comfortable to stand close to the counter. Most people prefer a countertop height of 36 in. (Shorter or taller people may prefer a countertop that is lower or higher.) If your countertop is 1½ in. thick, make the cabinets 34½ in. tall, including the toekick; adjust the cabinet height if the countertop is thinner or thicker. Most base cabinets are about 24 in. deep with a 25-in.-deep countertop that overhangs the cabinet by about 1 in.

An 18-in. vertical space between the countertop and the bottom of the wall cabinet is good for installing under-cabinet lights that will illuminate the countertop without shining in people's eyes.

CABINET DIMENSIONS

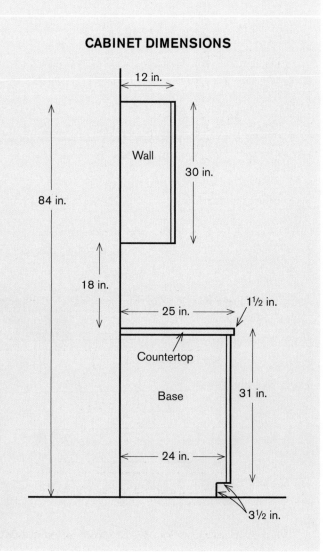

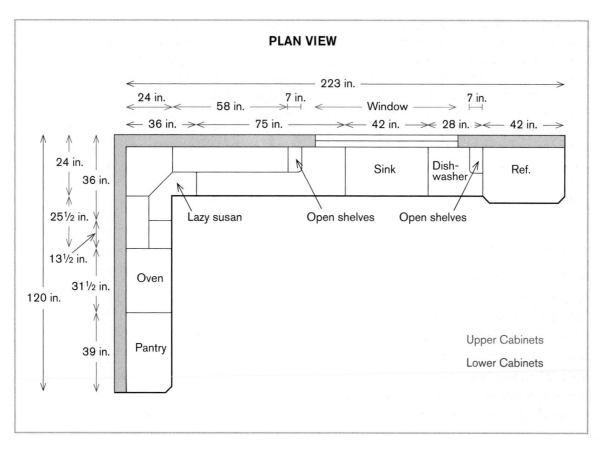

PLAN VIEW

223 in.

24 in.   58 in.   7 in.   Window   7 in.

36 in.   75 in.   42 in.   28 in.   42 in.

24 in.

36 in.

25½ in.

13½ in.

31½ in.

120 in.

39 in.

Oven

Pantry

Lazy susan

Open shelves

Open shelves

Sink

Dish-washer

Ref.

Upper Cabinets

Lower Cabinets

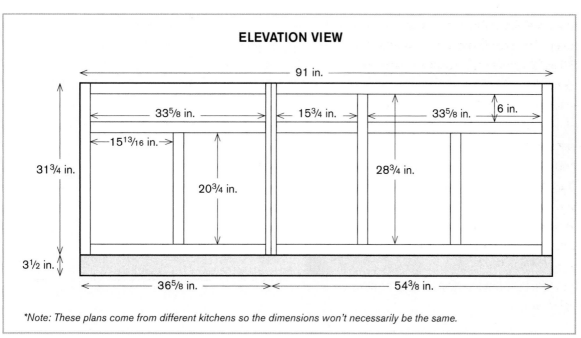

ELEVATION VIEW

91 in.

33⅝ in.   15¾ in.   33⅝ in.   6 in.

15¹³⁄₁₆ in.

31¾ in.

20¾ in.

28¾ in.

3½ in.

36⅝ in.   54⅜ in.

Note: These plans come from different kitchens so the dimensions won't necessarily be the same.

Door and Drawer Face Options

By far the most visible parts of the cabinets will be the doors and the drawer faces. Some types are much more difficult to make than others. So choose the style, materials, and finish that please you but also make sure you will be able to build them—lots of them—in a reasonable amount of time and without having to spend too much money on new tools.

END PANELS

End panels, which cover the sides of cabinets where they will be visible, are sometimes made to mimic the look of doors—and they're made in much the same way. However, some people prefer plain end panels even when the cabinet doors are built more decoratively.

Visit a kitchen store to see a wide selection of door styles, wood species, and finishes.

Drawer faces are usually attached to the face of a drawer body after the body has been built. Drawer faces are sometimes built to match the style of doors, for a uniform kitchen style. However, in some kitchens, drawer faces are simpler—for instance, doors may be made with rails and stiles, while drawer faces are plain 1 × slabs, perhaps with a routed edge detail.

SLAB STYLE

The simplest doors are just slabs, with no frames or detailing. Many people appreciate their clean lines. Adding decorative pulls or knobs may provide all the visual interest they want.

To make slab doors and faces, use high-quality plywood or melamine board or other stock that is dry and unlikely to warp; if you do that, your doors should remain warp-free for decades. To further ensure against warping, you may choose to add two or more horizontal cleats to the back side of the door.

These, of course, are the easiest doors to build. If you choose to go with slabs, you can build your kitchen cabinets using only a tablesaw—or even just a circular saw with a reliable guide. The cut edges of the slabs can be covered with edge-banding or you may choose to frame the slabs with thin strips of wood.

Slab doors made of stained hardwood plywood feel modern yet cozy.

These slab doors can be quickly made with white melamine board—as long as you are able to make very straight cuts in sheet goods.

HARDWARE OPTIONS

The knobs or pulls you choose go a long way toward defining the look of your cabinets. Knobs can recede visually or they can make a stunning statement. Styles range from old-fashioned to a casual cottage look to sleek and European.

These doors are made with Shaker frames and ¼-in. plywood panels. Straightforward crown molding at the top completes the look.

These cabinets have routed stiles and rails as well as raised panels.

FRAME-AND-PANEL DOORS

The most common door type is composed of a panel surrounded by a frame. The frame's two vertical members are called the stiles, and the two horizontals are the rails.

Plywood panels. Panels may be made of plywood, which is most often ¼ in. thick. Plywood panels, which are commonly used for economical cabinets you can buy at home centers, are inexpensive and easy to make. You simply cut the panels to size. Doors made with plywood panels are light, but if constructed carefully they can certainly be durable. And many people prefer their sleek, more modern look to that of raised panels.

Raised panels. The raised panels shown in the photo at right are made with ¾-in.-thick material, shaped so the edges fit into the ¼-in.-thick grooves in the stiles and rails. If the door will be painted, it can be made of a sheet of medium-density fiberboard (MDF). If it will be stained, pieces of hardwood are glued edge to edge to make up a panel.

Raised panels are something of a challenge to make. Before you can edge-glue wood pieces together, the edges must be perfectly straight or gaps will appear where they join. Even straight-looking dimensional lumber is rarely straight enough. So you will need to run the edges of the boards through a jointer or perhaps a router table specially equipped for jointing. Unless your boards are perfectly flat, they should be run through a modest-size thickness planer. Once the pieces are glued together, the surface will need to be smoothed. Depending on how precisely the boards are joined, you may need only to sand them smooth. Or you may need to run them through an extra-wide thickness planer, which is a very expensive machine.

Rails and stiles. Frames made with very simple rails and stiles can be produced using a tablesaw, but most frame types require a good-quality variable-speed router of at least 2¼ hp, a router table, and specially matched bits to produce the grooves in the sides, so the four frame pieces and the panel can fit together.

Shaker-style doors have simple square-looking rails and stiles. A modified Shaker style has a frame that is square cut on its outside edges but is slightly chamfered (or beveled) on the inside, so it collects less dust.

COTTAGE STYLE

If rustic, shabby chic, or homey is the look you're after, building drawers and drawer faces can be pretty straightforward. You don't want them to look sloppy, but joints can be a bit more casual. Cottage-style doors often use two or three horizontal cleats on each door; the cleats are usually on the back side, but could be on the front for an even more rustic look. The vertical boards are sometimes tongue and groove, which you could buy or make yourself using a router table.

This door has a Shaker-style look, but it is modified with a chamfered inside edge, which makes it easier to keep clean.

The darker stain along the outside edge of the door panels makes this kitchen seem formal and dignified.

Cottage-style doors often use tongue-and-groove joinery. These doors are held together with cleats on the back.

Thick cross-reeded textured glass obscures the dinnerware inside and creates a memorable look.

GLASS DOORS

You may want to show off some of your glassware or dinnerware with glass doors; glass opens up a kitchen and makes it feel more spacious. Doors with glass inserts are not difficult to build and can be made to suit a variety of styles. Most people prefer to have only a couple of doors with glass; they don't want to make every cabinet a window display that they have to keep neat. It's common to use the same frame pieces as on the other doors, but simpler frames usually do not look out of place. Obscure or textured glass (including seeded, ribbed, cross-reeded, and frosted) lessens the need for neatly organized shelves.

Cabinet Configurations

In addition to choosing the door and drawer face style, there are two more basic cabinet choices to make: whether you will build frameless or face-frame cabinets and whether the doors and drawer faces will be overlaid or inset in the cabinets.

FRAME OR FRAMELESS?

There are two basic ways to build cabinet cases (also called carcases): with or without a face frame. Which you choose depends on your skills and tools and, to a certain extent, on the look you want, although when the doors are closed the two types can look very similar.

Face frame. A face-frame cabinet is constructed of sheet goods with a frame in front, usually made of 1½-in.-wide hardwood. Because plywood or melamine sheets are usually ¾ in. thick, the frames overlap the sheets by ¼ in. on the inside and the outside. Door hinges are mounted on the frame rather than on the sheet goods.

Face-frame cabinets are perhaps the most common type in this country. Here are some reasons for that:

- Because the frames run past the case on the outside, they can be planed or sanded to fit if a small error is made or if a wall is wavy.

- Some people feel that the frame adds needed strength and rigidity to a cabinet.

- Though sheet goods should always be cut straight and clean, a face frame will cover very small blemishes in the cut.

There are, however, some downsides:

- Because the frame is wider than the side of the cabinet, access to the inside of the cabinet is slightly limited.

- Face frames necessitate narrower drawers. A typical frame overlays the inside of the cabinet by ½ in., which means the drawer will be 1 in. narrower than one installed on a frameless cabinet.

- Hardwood frames are fairly pricey—or very pricey, if you use cherry or another high-end wood.

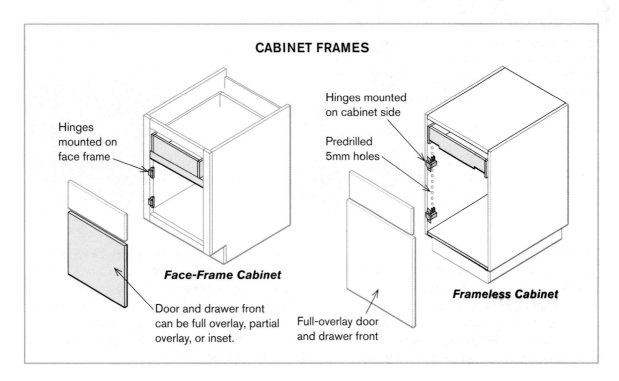

CABINET FRAMES

Hinges mounted on face frame

Hinges mounted on cabinet side

Predrilled 5mm holes

Face-Frame Cabinet

Frameless Cabinet

Door and drawer front can be full overlay, partial overlay, or inset.

Full-overlay door and drawer front

These cabinets are made with a face frame that is visible at the bottom only; aside from the bottom, they are indistinguishable from frameless cabinets.

Frameless. Also known as Euro-style, frameless cabinets are built in the same way as frame cabinets, but without the frame. The face of the case is covered with glued-on edge-banding instead of wood strips.

Some folks are leery of frameless cabinetry, but it is gaining in popularity for several reasons:

- It is economical because you don't need to buy hardwood for the trim.

- Access to the inside of the cabinet is not limited by a frame.

- It has been proved strong enough in most situations. One possible exception: a cabinet wider than 36 in. that is freestanding—that is, not wedged between cabinets or a wall on each side. However, frameless cabinets are plenty strong in the typical kitchen setup because the ends of horizontal members are tightly captured between the verticals and therefore almost never sag.

- Assuming you install doors and drawer faces that are overlaid, faceless cabinets look almost exactly the same as framed cabinets once the doors are closed.

- In the past, hinges that are attached to the sheet goods rather than to a wood frame had a tendency to pull out. But with today's hardware, even hinges attached to particleboard or MDF will stay strong.

Here are some possible downsides:

- To make frameless cabinets, you must have confidence in your ability to cut the front edges precisely straight and clean, without even tiny chips, because the edge-banding will not always hide imperfections.

- Cabinets must be correctly sized because there are no frames to plane or sand for minor adjustments. However, frameless cabinets are typically installed with a space left open near the wall, which can be filled with a strip of wood. This strip of wood can accommodate those minor adjustments.

The projects in this book are pretty evenly divided between frameless and face-frame cabinetry.

OVERLAY AND INSET OPTIONS

You must also decide how much of the cabinet case or frame the doors and drawer faces will cover. The basic options are as follows:

- A full overlay door is the most common type of door nowadays. This style covers the frame or case edge almost completely, so you see only the doors and drawer faces when they are closed.

- A partial overlay door is used for face-frame cabinets only. This style typically exposes 1 in. of the (horizontal) rails and 2 in. of the (vertical) stiles, but you may choose to expose more or less of the rails and/or stiles. Older versions of partial overlay doors had rabbets cut around the perimeter to create a lip, so the door sat partway inside the opening.

- Inset doors are set inside frame or frame-less cabinets. This creates a vintage look that many people like. There is typically a ⅛-in. gap between the door and the case or frame. Inset doors must be precisely cut to fit; even tiny imperfections will scream for attention. For that reason, they are usually built to be a bit too large, and then are cut to size just before installing. In this style, hinges, or at least the hinge pins, are visible.

Inset doors are a bit tricky to achieve but create a look with old-fashioned appeal.

Partially overlaid doors expose part of the door frame, for a slightly more traditional appearance.

WALL CABINET HEIGHTS

Of course, the taller the cabinet, the more you can store in it. But all of a 30-in.-tall wall cabinet's shelves will be accessible to an adult of average height. If cabinets are 36 in. or 42 in. tall, people may need a stepstool to get at the top shelves—not a problem if the uppermost items are rarely needed.

CORNER POSSIBILITIES

An inside corner is often treated with an angled wall cabinet and two straight base cabinets, as shown in the photo on the facing page. An angled wall cabinet improves accessible space, especially if you add a lazy susan. It is also possible to install an angled corner base cabinet, but that can create

tip

The kitchen floor may be installed first, in which case you will want to protect it with heavy cardboard while installing the cabinets. Or you can install the cabinets so they rest on top of temporary pieces that are the same thickness as the future floor. Once the cabinets are in place, you can then install the flooring, slipping it under the cabinets.

SETTING ON TOP

A base cabinet can be made with full-height vertical sheets that rest on the floor. In that case, the sheets will be cut with a notch at the bottom to accommodate the toekick. Another method, used in this book, is to build a simple box that is 3½ in. shorter than the cabinet will be and to install it on a frame made of 2×4s that rest on the floor. Or the box can be set on adjustable legs (see p. 108). Either the 2×4 frame or the legs are covered with 1×4 finish pieces for a neat-looking toekick.

BASIC BOX ON TOP OF 2×4 TOEKICK

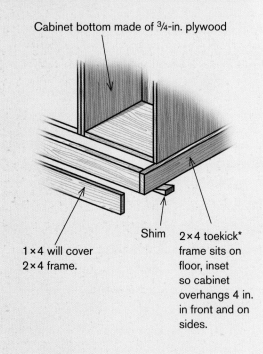

Cabinet bottom made of ¾-in. plywood

1×4 will cover 2×4 frame.

Shim

2×4 toekick* frame sits on floor, inset so cabinet overhangs 4 in. in front and on sides.

Note: Toekick will be installed 4 in. back from cabinet's front edge.

If there is no soffit, the space above the cabinets can be used for display.

A large, glass, angled wall cabinet turns a difficult storage space into a display asset.

difficulties for the countertop, which must then be angled as well—and therefore must be wider than usual, which can be quite expensive. The space in the base cabinet corner can be made more accessible with the addition of pullout shelving like that shown on p. 178.

CABINETS ABOVE APPLIANCES

You will almost certainly need to design and build two or more wall cabinets that fit above a range hood, refrigerator, or other appliance. If, like most people, you want the tops of all the cabinets to be at the same height, have the appliance or at least its literature on hand when you design.

Many range hoods are only a few inches tall, while others with microwaves can be 16 in. or taller. A range hood typically vents to the outside, which probably means you'll need to cut a hole in the cabinet to make room for the ducts.

Above a refrigerator you may choose to have a cabinet that fits snugly, with only 1 in. or 2 in. of clearance. Or you may want more space, so you can use the fridge top as a shelf.

ISLANDS

If your kitchen is wider than 10 ft., you probably have room for an island. Make sure there is ample space—at least 3 ft., and preferably 4 ft. or more—on all sides, so there will not be a traffic bottleneck.

A simple island can be as narrow as 24 in. If you have more space, have the countertop overhang to create a bar for eating. If you choose to include a cooktop, choose a model with its own downdraft vent fan; you will need to run gas pipe or a 220-volt electrical line for the cooktop as well as ductwork through the floor.

The cabinetry can mimic the rest of the kitchen, or you may choose to create a one-of-a-kind statement

In this kitchen, wall cabinets of different heights fit above appliances, creating a useful and attractive custom kitchen.

A kitchen island must be finished on all four sides. If the countertop overhangs by 12 in. or more, it can also be used as an eating station. This large island contains plenty of storage space.

COVE LIGHTING

If you leave space between the wall cabinets and the ceiling, consider installing cove lighting. This can be inexpensive fluorescent or other fixtures; the fixtures will not be visible. Cove lighting shines gracefully up at the ceiling and bounces off it to provide gentle ambient lighting for the whole kitchen.

A modest amount of open shelving can perk up a kitchen's appearance, adding interest to the overall design.

piece. Side panels are often the most visible, while the backside is often not as visible and can be plainer. If the island is longer than 3 ft., it is usually best to make it out of two attached cabinets.

OPEN SHELVES

Open shelves make it mighty easy to get at stuff; they open up a small space and they can enliven a design by adding a new feature. Shelves with no doors are, of course, easier to build than a cabinet with doors. Many kitchens benefit from a bit of open shelving, but keep it limited: It can be difficult to keep your kitchen display-worthy at all times.

CROWN MOLDING

If your cabinets do not butt up against a soffit, topping them off with crown molding will give the kitchen a unified look. Choose molding made of the same material as the cabinets and in a style that harmonizes with them. Crown molding is usually easier to install on top of cabinets than at the top of a wall, because you don't have to contend with the ceiling. Still, this is pretty serious trimwork, so careful planning, making test cuts, and an accurate chopsaw are needed.

Crown molding gives this kitchen an upscale feel and ties together a series of wall cabinets into a unified whole.

2 tools

THIS BOOK shows you how to build a wide range of cabinets. Of course, if you have an extensive collection of pro-level tools and a large shop, work will proceed smoothly and you will have many design options. But I'll also show you how good-quality cabinets can be built with a modest collection of tools.

Buy the best-quality tools you can afford. Sometimes the best value is in used high-quality tools rather than new middle- or low-quality tools. But always consult with woodworkers or knowledgeable salespeople and take tools for a test-drive whenever possible. Stationary tools should hum rather than rattle and should remain stable while being used; fences and baseplates should be flat and even. Hand tools should be comfortable to hold, easy to adjust, and feel solid with no loose parts.

Unless the weather is predictably good enough to set up outside, establish an indoor workshop that is as spacious as possible. Then organize it so it will be easy to keep clean. Assign often-used small tools to predictable and easy-to-reach shelves, racks, or drawers, so you spend as little time as possible looking for them.

Stationary Shop Tools

Good-quality shop tools make many of the operations in this book easier. If you have room, put them where you can use them right away; if not, make them easy to access. Take the time to place them on firm surfaces and test their operations so they will cut or bore accurately.

TABLESAW

An accurate tablesaw is the foundation of most woodworking shops, enabling you to make straight cuts in sheet goods quickly. A professional-quality model is a great thing to have, but even a good-quality contractor's work-site tablesaw can be used for making cabinets.

A good tablesaw uses a 10-in. blade or larger. Adjustments for height and bevel should operate smoothly. Whether stationary or mounted on a collapsible stand, it should rest firmly and not move while you cut.

The tables and supports surrounding a tablesaw are as important as the saw itself. To make clean, long cuts, you should have plenty of outfeed support—a table or other support (some have wheels) that will keep the sheet from falling when you finish the cut. To cut full-width sheets, have plenty of support on at least one side of the blade.

Give a tablesaw plenty of room in your shop, so a helper can finish pulling a full sheet all the way through during a rip cut.

If you will use the tablesaw to make crosscuts, you could simply use the rip fence along with the saw's sliding miter gauge. But for greater ease and accuracy, build a sled, as shown on pp. 146–148.

This tablesaw has a large work surface with plenty of side and outfeed support as well as a solid rip fence, making it fairly easy to cut large sheets accurately.

This rip fence locks down securely. Its width gauge can be precisely adjusted so it can dependably and accurately measure the width of a cut.

Use a straightedge to check that the saw's table and any adjoining tables are nice and flat in all directions.

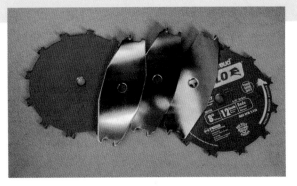

A dado blade set enables a tablesaw to cut wide grooves.

A professional-quality tablesaw is a great tool for cabinetry. However, a modest contractor's tablesaw can also be used, as long as the fence and crosscut guide are accurate, the table is flat, and the blade is sharp. The saw shown here was used to make many of the projects in this book.

tip

Using the correct tablesaw blade for the job will help you make smooth cuts. For hardwood or softwood lumber, use a combination blade with at least 50 teeth. For plywood, particleboard, and MDF, use a blade with 80 teeth or more. If you plan to cut melamine sheets, use a blade made specifically for that purpose.

POWER MITER SAW

Also called a chopsaw, a power miter saw is a portable tool that deserves a permanent place in your shop. A good power miter saw is essential for achieving professional results because it easily makes precise clean cuts in seconds.

A 10-in. saw handles all but the widest trim boards; an 8-in. saw will limit the width of boards you can cut. (Remember that cutting at 45° angles calls for more cutting width.)

Grab the handle and move the saw from side to side to be sure there will be no wobble while in use. Equip it with a new or newly sharpened carbide-tipped blade with at least 50 teeth.

A standard miter saw with no bevel option (which is what some people mean by chopsaw) is ideal for cutting rails and stiles, most crown molding, and

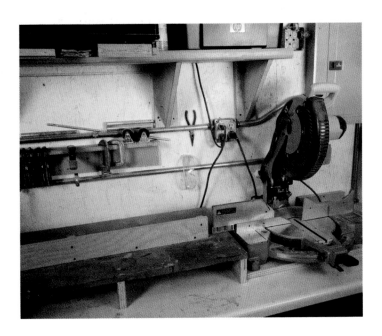

Firmly attached to a bench and fitted with an adjoining table with fence, a standard power miter saw becomes a serious shop tool.

ENSURE GREAT CUTS

It's well worth your time to make sure your saw makes precise cuts *before* you start cutting into the wood you've bought for cabinetmaking. To do so, cut a scrap piece of wood with your miter saw, then flip one of the cut sides over and press it against the other cut. If the cuts are at an exact 90° angle, they should meet perfectly, as shown at right.

Use the same test to be sure the saw cuts at an exact right angle through the board's thickness: The ends should meet perfectly along their thickness. If not, consult your user's manual and make adjustments until your saw is reliably accurate.

other trim pieces. For the projects in this book, a standard saw is all you need, though some pros use a bevel (or compound miter) feature to cut crown molding.

Depending on its size, a sliding miter saw may be able to crosscut 12-in.-wide sheets for wall cabinets but not the wider sheets used for base cabinets.

Bolt the miter saw firmly to a workbench, and set up a table with a fence on at least one side, as shown on the facing page.

RADIAL-ARM SAW

A radial-arm saw occupies a groove midway between a tablesaw and a miter saw. Cheaper models are wobbly and unreliable, but better radial-arm saws can make accurate crosscuts up to 12 in. or so in width. Test yours and make adjustments before using it for cabinet work.

Fitted with a flat table and a straight fence, a good-quality radial-arm saw is a useful addition to a shop.

ROUTER AND ROUTER TABLE

There's no need for a plunge router when making kitchen cabinets. However, you do need a powerful router—at least 2¼ hp. And it needs to be variable speed because you must run it at slower speeds for wider bits (for example, see p. 154). Most if not all of your routing will be done on a router table.

A router is typically used for cutting rabbets and dadoes. Using matched bit sets, it is indispensable for cutting the special grooves in door rails and stiles that are needed to fit them together and to fit the panel as well (see chapter 8).

Some router tables can also be used for jointing—straightening the edges of boards so they can snug up against each other to make multiboard panels (see p. 61).

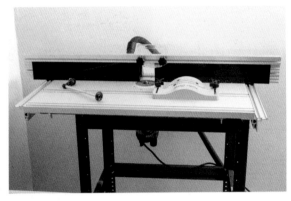

This Sommerfeld router table, equipped with a Triton router, is more expensive than other brands but has a couple of features that make it easy to use: Router bits can be raised and lowered using a crank from above and bits can be quickly changed using a single wrench from above.

When making most types of frame-and-panel cabinet doors, you need a variable-speed router that is at least 2¼ hp.

This shopmade router table is made with melamine, which is supported so it stays nice and flat. A router baseplate fits snugly in a cutout in the middle. The fence, which is held in place with clamps, is simply made of straight pieces of wood and has a port for dust collection.

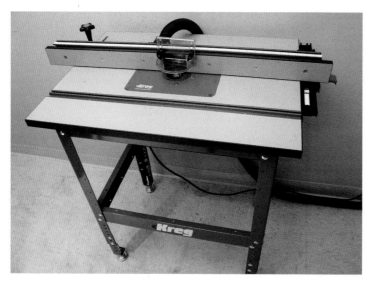

This Kreg router table has some advantages over a home-made one: The dust collector works better, especially with the guard in place. The fence is easier to adjust, and it has a feature that allows you to use it for jointing.

tip

Some professional woodworking shops have a tool called a shaper. A typical shaper is fairly humongous and can cut deep grooves in hard-woods with ease, whereas sometimes you need to make two or more passes with a router table to complete a groove. However, because the blade on a shaper spins slowly, a shaper is actually less useful for making the smaller grooves often called for when building kitchen cabinets; the higher spinning speed of a router creates smoother cuts. So most woodworkers today choose a router over a shaper.

CHANGING BITS

For some operations—such as routing many types of rails and stiles for doors—you will need to change router bits often. With some router table setups this can be time-consuming and tedious, as you kneel under or hunch over the table to get at the nut.

Triton makes a router for which you can change the bits above the table. Use a crank to raise or lower the bit and use a single wrench—while pushing a locking mechanism under the table—to remove and replace a bit, as shown on the Sommerfeld table below left.

A lower-tech solution is to simply hang your router in place rather than screwing it down; in most cases, the router is heavy enough to stay put on its own. Now you can lift the router up and out to change the bits, as shown below right.

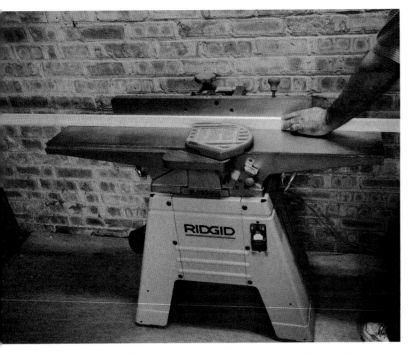

Use a jointer to produce perfectly straight and smooth board edges.

A jointer quickly adjusts to remove a little or a lot. In most cases, you will not remove more than 1/8 in. at a pass.

JOINTER

A jointer is essentially a power planer under-mounted to a flat metal base. Use it to straighten the edges of rough-cut boards or to remove bows and other imperfections. When making hardwood raised door panels, you will need to glue up two or more boards edge to edge, which can be done only if the edges are perfectly straight. To get those perfectly straight edges, a jointer is needed.

However, you may not need a jointer. If, for instance, your doors will have plywood panels, there will be no need to glue boards together. And if you carefully choose dimensional lumber (rather than lumber with one or more rough edge), the edges may be straight enough to make rails and stiles.

OTHER OPTIONS FOR JOINTING

You may be able to do a fair amount of jointing work using a tablesaw (pp. 146–148) or a router table (p. 61). However, if you have lots of hardwood jointing to do, a jointer is probably worth the investment.

Some old-fashioned woodworkers use long handplanes for jointing. If you have strong arms and not much jointing to do, you may want to try this.

If you need to joint only the narrow boards used for cabinet or door rails and stiles, you may be able to use a thickness planer; many can be adjusted to joint edges of boards up to 6 in. wide.

THICKNESS PLANER

If your boards are not all smooth and of uniform thickness—as is often the case with hardwoods—a thickness planer is a very useful tool. Start feeding a board into a thickness planer, and the tool will do the rest, slowly pulling the board on rollers while its cutters smooth one side at a time.

Many inexpensive portable thickness planers work well and reduce thickness efficiently. And, as mentioned in "Other Options for Jointing," on the facing page, many thickness planers can also be used as a jointer for boards 6 in. or narrower.

DRILL PRESS

Many drill presses are surprisingly affordable—and surprisingly versatile as well. With this tool you can make holes that are sure to be straight, whereas hand drilling inevitably produces holes at various angles to the face of the board. Use a drill press for boring the partial-depth holes needed for Euro-style hinges and to make a series of holes for adjustable shelving.

To position one or a series of holes at the correct distance from a board's end, you can quickly modify a drill press's fence by placing a board of the correct width against it. Or you may choose to build an adjustable fence of your own, using a board held in place with clamps.

A 13-in. thickness planer is modestly priced and can smooth and straighten individual boards. If you need to plane wider glued-up panels, a much more expensive planer is needed.

Even a modest drill press is easy to use and ensures straight holes.

tip

Many inexpensive thickness planers can handle boards up to 13 in. wide. That works for most individual boards. However, if you glue up two or more boards for a door panel, you may end up with a panel that is too wide for your machine. Unfortunately, wider thickness planers jump in price dramatically—from hundreds to thousands of dollars. Unless you have that kind of money or chance upon a good used wide thickness planer, the solution is usually to glue up very carefully, so the edges line up as close to perfect as you can get. Then use hand tools—a power sander, a scraper, and/or a hand sander—to smooth the panel. See p. 150 for this operation.

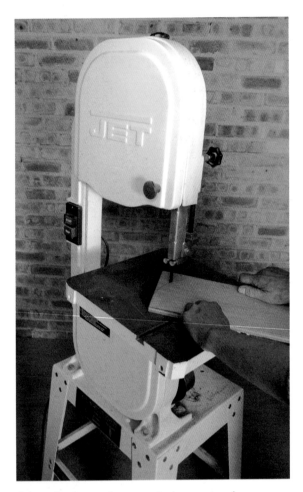

A **bandsaw** may be mounted on a stand, as shown, or it can rest on a workbench.

BANDSAW

Curved cuts are occasionally called for when making kitchen cabinets, open shelves, or adjoining trim pieces. You can usually cut these items using a handheld jigsaw, but a bandsaw ensures that the curved cut will be at a right angle to the face of the board—something that can be difficult to achieve with a jigsaw. A bandsaw also makes it easier to follow curved lines with the blade, which is fully visible as you work. A bandsaw is not necessary for most cabinetry, but you may be surprised at the low price of many models, and it is a useful addition to a shop.

DUST COLLECTION

Cutting, sanding, and routing create plenty of sawdust, some of it in the form of chips and large particles, and lots of it as a fine dust that settles over everything, worms its way through doors and windows, and gets into all available nooks and crannies. Fortunately, there are a number of dust-collection options that can greatly cut down on the powdery stuff.

The best dust collection is a large two-stage system with a powerful motor, which takes up plenty of space and costs plenty of money. Ideally it should be hooked up to solid rather than flexible ducting and should have a number of ducts that extend permanently to the ports of various shop tools. If you have the room and money for such a system, by all means get one.

Smaller and cheaper systems can also remove significant portions of dust. Some types attach to

This inexpensive dust collection system attaches to a shop vacuum, which you probably already own.

A vent fan like this shuttles dusty air to the outside.

This dust collector has a feature that cleans the filter with the push of a button, so you rarely need to remove it. It has a powerful motor that sucks away up to 99% of the dust. You can wheel it near the tool or keep it in one place and use a long hose.

the shop vacuum that you already own, while others have their own motors. Cyclone units work nearly as well as two-stage systems to capture small dust particles. With a less-expensive system, you will probably need to move the hose to attach it to each individual tool.

Handheld Tools

Handheld tools for cabinetry don't need to be top-of-the-line professional models, but avoid the cheapest tools. Mid-range tools sold at a home center will almost always do the job. When possible, try out a tool first or ask someone knowledgeable before making a purchase.

CIRCULAR SAW

Woodworkers most often use a 7¼-in. circular saw to make rough cuts in sheet goods before precisely cutting with a tablesaw. If the circular saw cuts cleanly and you use a reliable rip guide, you can even use it to make finish cuts in sheets (see p. 55). Equip a circular saw with a finish-cutting blade that has at least 40 teeth; for cutting melamine, use a blade made especially for that.

A good mid-priced circular saw and a jigsaw, once equipped with the right blades and operated with care, can make many of the cuts needed for cabinet work.

Before cutting, check that a circular saw's blade is straight to the baseplate. If not, it can be easily adjusted.

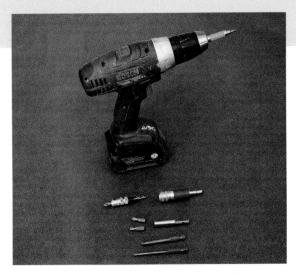

Outfit your cordless drill with a quick-change driver to fit all the screws you will use. Square-drive trim-head screws are the most common type used.

DRILL

A 14-volt, 18-volt, or 20-volt cordless drill comes in handy for boring pilot and pocket holes and for driving screws. It should have a charger and an extra battery, so you can always be ready to bore or drive. A quick-change magnetic setup allows you to change easily from boring to driving and holds screws on the bit as you work. For attaching cabinets with screws, have combination counter-sink/counterbore bits as well as square-drive or Phillips® bits.

POWER SANDERS

A random-orbit sander is the sanding tool of choice among many woodworkers. It has a pad that allows you to quickly change sandpapers as you progress though the grits—60-grit or 80-grit paper for removing a good deal of material, then medium grits (100 and 120), and finally 180-grit or 220-grit paper for final smoothing. A random-orbit sander can get into edges and crannies with ease and will not dig into the wood, which produces divots.

If you make raised panels that are too wide for your thickness planer, a belt sander can be useful for initial smoothing. Use it carefully and hold it flat to the surface, to avoid making waves in the panel.

DOWEL JIG

One way to invisibly attach two boards is with dowels, short wood pegs that fit into matching holes in both boards. A dowel jig helps you drive straight and perfectly aligned dowel holes in two boards. There are many types of dowel jigs. Choose one that will allow you to drill two or more holes at a time in a board, to minimize setup time. For information on how to make a dowel joint with minimal tools, see pp. 75–77.

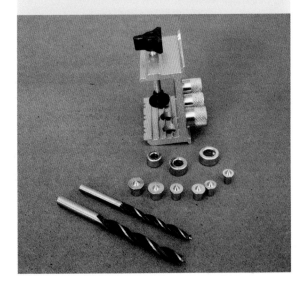

A random-orbit sander handles most jobs, but occasionally you may need a belt sander for heavy-duty sanding.

To be ready for any smoothing or evening job, maintain a stock of various sandpapers and sanding blocks as well as a plane and a scraper.

HAND SANDERS, PLANES, AND SCRAPERS

Many woodworkers use hand sanders for the final smoothing because it gives them more control and they can move with the grain. Use a drywall-type sander for large, flat surfaces, a smaller block sander for smaller flat areas, and a sponge sander or simply a handheld piece of sandpaper for curves and niches.

A simple wood scraper is surprisingly effective at removing material and initially smoothing uneven boards, and a handplane is useful for shaving the edges of frame pieces.

POWER NAILERS

Hand-nailing is slow work; driving trim-head screws is easier. You can quickly secure cabinet cases with wood glue and a power trim nailer or stapler. A brad nailer drives nails long enough for rabbeted joints.

HANDY TAPE MEASURE

This FastCap® woodworker's tape has highly visible markings for sixteenths of an inch—dimensions that often come up during cabinetmaking. It has an erasable notepad on the side, and even incorporates a pencil sharpener.

A trim or brad nailer drives screws that are nearly invisible. A stapler's fasteners are definitely visible, but they're strong.

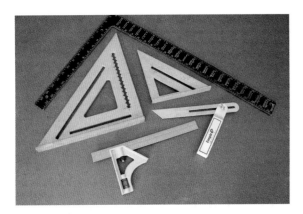

A collection of squares is handy for keeping things at 90° or 45°. A T-bevel helps duplicate other angles.

A biscuit joiner cuts slots for inserting biscuits, which make for a strong invisible joint.

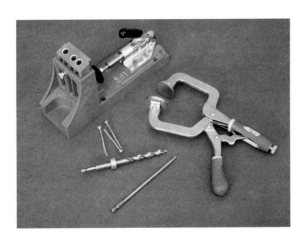

SQUARES

You will continually check for square as you work, because driving even one fastener while a cabinet is misaligned will make it permanently imperfect. In addition to a framing square, keep on hand a small and large Speed® Square to check quickly for square, a sliding combination square to check in tight spots and to make quick measurements, and a T-bevel for capturing and marking odd angles.

BISCUIT JOINER

Also called a plate joiner, a biscuit joiner slices slots in the edges or faces of mating boards. The slots and fitted biscuits are glued and clamped together, producing an invisible and very strong joint. Because biscuits are fairly wide, you can use them only for boards 3 in. or wider.

POCKET-HOLE JIGS

Pocket-hole joinery (see pp. 64–65) has become very popular among woodworkers because it produces strong joints quickly. Professional cabinet shops have dedicated pocket-hole machines that produce multiple slots in an instant, but more modest jigs, like those made by Kreg, enable you to cut slots and assemble boards almost as quickly.

CLAMPS

Clamps are essential to cabinetry. You will use them to hold together a number of doors or drawer faces at a time as well as to make face frames and hold cabinet cases together while you fasten them. So have a collection of various types and sizes on hand. Pipe clamps are most commonly used, but bar clamps, squeeze clamps, and others often come in handy as well.

There are various types of pocket-hole jigs. All make it easy to fasten boards and sheets invisibly yet strongly.

Many woodworkers find pipe clamps to be the most useful clamps in their shop. Keep a variety of other clamps on hand so you can quickly handle most any situation.

The Kreg Automaxx™ Bench Klamp System™ holds boards down firmly while you work. The Auto-Adjust feature means you don't have to adjust the clamp for different thicknesses of boards.

FINISH SPRAYERS

An inexpensive airless sprayer can work well for painting walls or fences, but its spray is not smooth enough for cabinetry. You want a sprayer that adequately atomizes the finish material.

One way to get that perfectly stipple-free finish is with a high-volume, low-pressure (HVLP) sprayer. Conversion-type HVLPs must connect to a powerful (80 gal. or more) compressor; a small compressor for a set of nail guns will not power it. Another type of HPLV sprayer uses a turbine, which is a series of fans that moves air through the spray gun. These setups tend to be fairly expensive.

A low-volume, low-pressure (LVLP) sprayer is a much less-expensive option, especially if you

already own a small compressor. The gun itself can cost $100 to $200. Some professionals report that their LVLP sprayer achieves great-looking finishes for far less cost than an HVLP.

tip Some finishes can be applied by hand, either with a roller, brush, or rag. The results can have professional-quality smoothness or a homemade charm, depending on the method (see p. 165).

An inexpensive LVLP sprayer can be hooked up to a small compressor.

An HVLP sprayer with a turbine unit is easy to use but a bit pricey.

3 wood

Most hardwood plywood has a very thin hardwood veneer on each side and interior plies made of softer woods.

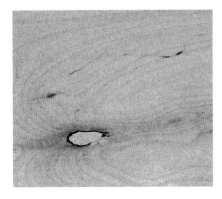

The back side of this sheet of plywood has some blemishes as well as a filled knot.

CABINET CASES and some doors and drawer faces are made of sheet goods, such as plywood, particleboard, MDF, and melamine-coated sheets. If a case will have a face frame, hardwood is used for that. Hardwood is also used for the frames around doors and drawer fronts. Thin ¼-in. plywood can be used for door panels. If door panels are raised, they are usually made of glued-up hardwood boards, though MDF can be used if the door will be painted. All but oversize drawer bodies have bottoms made of ¼-in. plywood; drawer sides can be made of ½-in.-thick hardboard or a high-quality plywood (such as Baltic birch) that is ½ in. thick. The wood you use largely determines the look and quality of the cabinets, so spend some time choosing hardwoods and sheet goods that look great without busting your budget.

Sheet Goods

The sheets you will use to build cabinet cases and perhaps doors are composite, made of wood veneers, wood particles, and melamine veneers. Most but not all sheets are 4 ft. wide by 8 ft. long.

PLYWOOD

Plywood is composed of veneer sheets, or plies, cross-laminated with alternating grain patterns. This produces a material that is very strong for its weight and thickness (you will rarely see a karate demonstration that uses plywood, because it's nearly impossible to break cleanly). Standard plywood panels are made of three, five, or seven plies. Plywood does not shrink or break like standard lumber, but it can warp along its face if not stacked on a flat surface or attached firmly.

Plywood used for cabinetry usually has a hardwood veneer on each side. The face veneer is a good deal thinner than the core veneers, which are made of less-expensive wood. Hardwood plywood is available with a face veneer in nearly any wood species, meaning it can match most solid hardwoods in appearance.

You can sometimes couple less-expensive plywood with boards of another species. In particular, birch plywood can look much like maple and can be stained to look like cherry and other hardwoods.

OTHER CORES

Traditional plywood, often called "veneer-core" plywood, is fairly costly (which is why so many inexpensive cabinets are made of cheaper particleboard). In an effort to cut costs, many manufacturers make plywood that has an MDF core. You can also buy plywood with a particleboard core as well as plywood with a core that is partly wood veneer and partly MDF.

Cherry veneer with an MDF core.

EDGE-BANDINGS

Make sure you can get edge-banding for the plywood you choose. Iron-on banding is easiest to install. This store has a wide selection, but if you aren't able to find such a selection at a store near you check for online sources.

tip

Even if your plywood and hardwood are the same species, they may not look the same; colors within a species can vary considerably. Examine your sheets and boards carefully before buying.

Rotary-cut sheet with no seams.

MDF-core plywood sheets look the same on the outside as standard plywood and are available in a wide range of hardwood veneers. However, MDF is very heavy. Sheets made with a particleboard core are often the least expensive. They weigh less than MDF but are also less strong.

PLYWOOD GRADES, CUTS, AND MATCHING OPTIONS

The grades. Most plywood has one good side, which is graded with the letter A, B, or C, and a back side, which is graded with the number 1, 2, 3, or 4. So the top grade is A-1 and a middle grade board may be B-2. Typically, A-grade sheets have no knots—only tiny splits or burls; B grade has small knots and slightly visible burls and splits; and C grade has visible knots, splits, and burls.

The cut. Higher-grade top plies are cut in slices from the log. Depending on the orientation of the cut in relation to the wood grain, the result may be very narrow grain lines or a more variegated appearance, with wider grain lines in a wavy, pointed

BALTIC BIRCH PLYWOOD

While most hardwood plywoods have inner veneers made of softwood, all the plies in Baltic birch plywood are made of birch. Also, Baltic birch is made with no voids, so wherever you cut it there will be no little holes. This makes Baltic birch extra strong, and its cut edges, once sanded, are quite attractive.

Many cabinetmakers use ½-in. Baltic birch to make the sides of drawer bodies. The alternative—½-in.-thick hardwood—is more likely to warp and split. Drawer sides are generally narrow, so a single sheet of Baltic birch may be all you need for all your drawers.

Baltic birch is made in Europe and sometimes comes in metric sizes. But unlike most plywood, which is slightly thinner than its advertised thickness, ½-in. Baltic birch is a true ½ in. thick. Sheets are available in 5-ft. by 5-ft. and 4-ft. by 8-ft. sizes.

Rotary-cut flitches randomly placed.

PLYWOOD CUTS

- **Rotary cut.** The log is centered on a lathe and turned against a broad cutting knife set into the log at a slight angle.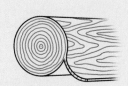

- **Quarter slicing.** The slicing is made perpendicular to the annual growth rings of the tree. This creates a straight grain appearance.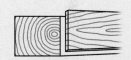

- **Lengthwise slicing.** This is done from a board of flatsawn lumber rather than from a log. A variegated figure is created with this slice.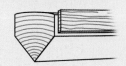

- **Plain slicing.** By slicing parallel to the center of the log, a raised "cathedral effect" is formed by the innermost growth rings.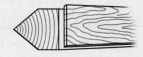

pattern. The illustrations in "Plywood Cuts" above show the effects created by various slicing orientations.

The least-expensive veneers are rotary cut, meaning the log is turned as if on a lathe against a wide cutting knife. The result is a veneer with wild grain patterns running in various directions.

Matching options. Slice-cut veneers are always less than 4 ft. wide, so a sheet will have seams where the veneer sections, called "flitches," meet. On a book-matched sheet (as shown in the near right photo), the flitches face each other to create a mirror image. If a sheet is slip matched (as shown in the far right photo), the flitches are side by side in a repeating pattern. In less-expensive sheets, flitches might be placed randomly.

Hickory veneer with book-matched flitches.

Slip-matched birch, with figures that seem to march in step.

MDF that is ¾ in. thick is often used for cabinet cases and doors that will be painted.

Particleboard is inexpensive and fragile, but can be useful in certain circumstances.

MDF

Medium-density fiberboard is made of wood fibers held together with wax and resin. It comes in 49-in. by 97-in. sheets and is brown-gray in color. MDF is inexpensive, easy to cut and shape, and holds screws fairly well, so it is often used for cabinet doors. As noted, some types of plywood have an MDF or partial MDF core.

There are some disadvantages, however: MDF is very heavy, which can make it difficult to work with, and although it is fairly hard, it tends to chip more easily than plywood. In addition, if it becomes wet, it can swell like a sponge with unattractive results. Still, many cabinetmakers use MDF; if you use it, take care to keep it well sealed with paint.

PARTICLEBOARD

Particleboard, also called chipboard, is made from wood chips and sawdust pressed into sheets with a resin. It is the least expensive of materials that can be used for cabinet cases.

Particleboard is hard, but not strong. It doesn't hold screws firmly (though newer types of fasten-

ers can anchor Euro-type hinges securely to it). It is easily chipped and will swell if exposed to water. Particleboard can be used for cabinet parts that will not be exposed to moisture but should not be used elsewhere.

MELAMINE SHEETS

Melamine is a hard, man-made product similar to the laminates used for countertops, although not as strong. An inexpensive alternative to plywood, melamine-coated particleboard (MCP) has a hard surface that does not need to be painted or finished and that resists moisture well. However, if the melamine coating is damaged or if moisture gets into the unprotected edges of the sheet, swelling will occur. Melamine sheets break as easily as plain particleboard sheets.

Melamine sheets are often used in cabinet-making, but special methods should be used and you'll need a melamine-cutting sawblade. Because melamine is too smooth to be glued to other surfaces, sheet edges should be rabbeted before attaching them together.

The MCP sheets shown here are white, but melamine is available in a range of colors.

Hardwoods

Many if not all of a cabinet's visible parts are typically made of hardwood: the door and drawer frames; the door and drawer panels, if they are raised; and the cabinet face frame, if there is one. Crown molding is also often made of hardwood molding, unless it will be painted, in which case MDF may be a better choice. (Other options are to make doors out of painted MDF, melamine, or reconstituted-wood sheets.) The wood and finish you choose will define the look of the cabinets.

SELECTING LUMBER

Unless you plan to paint your cabinets, you'll want to choose individual boards so as to get grain patterns and hues that harmonize. A typical home center or lumberyard may have a modest selection of poplar and oak, possibly maple, and perhaps a few more species. Their boards will likely be in standard dimensions (1×2, 1×3, 1×4, and so on) and in standard lengths (6 ft., 8 ft., 10 ft., and 12 ft.),

Some melamine mimics the look of natural wood, though imperfectly.

RECONSTITUTED-WOOD SHEETS

Reconstituted-wood veneer is made of natural rotary-cut wood veneer (often spruce, West African obeche, or poplar) that is colored with water-based dyes. The sheet cores may be made of MDF, chipboard, or wood plies.

These veneers come in a wide range of colors, patterns, and even textures. In many cases, the result is an uncanny resemblance to natural hardwood species, with a durable, easy-to-clean surface that needs no finishing or future refinishing. Often these sheets are less expensive than the hardwoods they imitate.

A hardwood specialty store may have as many as 25 wood species and subspecies on display.

PRECUT COMPONENTS

Some hardwood suppliers carry products that are precut and/or predrilled to save you time. If these are the right size for your projects, they're well worth the extra cost.

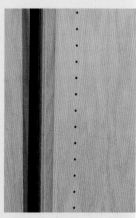

These precut drawer sides are made of Baltic birch, with precut grooves for drawer bottoms.

These plywood sheets are cut to width and pre-drilled with holes for adjustable shelving.

and all four sides and edges will be smooth. As long as they are straight (check them carefully), these boards can be easy to work with.

Other lumberyards may have a wider selection, and yards that specialize in hardwoods will have the widest array of wood types—often more than 20 species and subspecies. Their boards may be in random lengths and widths, and one or two of the edges may be rough cut, meaning you will have to rip-cut them on a good tablesaw.

Strolling the aisles of a hardwood yard can be fascinating and inspiring. But with greater choice comes greater work in selecting your wood.

- First choose both the species and perhaps the subspecies—for example, white oak. (You'll probably want to choose the finish at this point, so you know the final appearance.)

- Then, depending on availability, you may need to choose the cut—for instance, quartersawn or plainsawn.

- Finally, choose individual boards that are all similar in color and grain; some species can vary quite a bit.

This pinless moisture tester indicates a board's dryness level without poking holes in it. According to the tester, this board has some drying to do.

WOOD MUST BE DRY

Wood that is not sufficiently dried has a tendency to cup and warp, and maybe even crack or split. A moisture content of 8% to 14% is ideal for projects used indoors in rooms with normal levels of humidity. (If for some reason air humidity is above 75%, then the boards should have higher moisture content.) If you are buying from a reputable dealer or if the lumber is certified as kiln-dried with a label indicating moisture content, then your wood should be good to install.

But to be sure, or to test wood that you are unsure of, consider buying and using a moisture meter. Older meters had pins that poked into the wood, but newer meters do not mar the board as you test it.

Purchasing will be further complicated by the variety of available widths and lengths. For instance, you may be able to get four door stiles that are 32 in. long and 2 in. wide out of a board that is 65 in. long and 4½ in. wide. Be prepared to make calculations at the store.

tip

A tree's outer sapwood is often much lighter in color than its inner heartwood. Sapwood is also often less stable and more prone to warping, swelling, and splitting. Some boards are all sapwood or all heartwood, and others are a combination of the two.

HARDWOOD GRADES

Grades used for hardwoods are different from those used for softwoods. Here are some of the classifications you will find:

FAS. This stands for *firsts and seconds* and is the highest grade. It applies to boards 6 in. by 8 ft. and larger. Both faces of an FAS board are free of knots and other defects.

F1F. Also called "FAS one face," these boards meet FAS standards on one face only; the other face is no. 1 common or better.

Selects. This is almost the same as F1F but with a smaller minimum board length—those 4 in. by 6 ft. and larger.

Some boards bought at a hardwood store may have rough edges like this.

Prime. This is a more general grade but refers to boards of various sizes that are clear and free of visible defects.

No. 1 common. Sometimes called cabinet grade because it meets minimum standards for cabinet doors, this refers to boards 3 in. by 4 ft. and larger. Both faces of the board may have tiny knots and other very small blemishes, such as streaks and burls.

No. 2 common. These boards have more knots and blemishes. Use them if you find the knots and blemishes attractive.

HARDWOOD SPECIES

Though some people like the old-fashioned look of softwoods like pine or cedar, most cabinets are made of hardwood. Individual boards vary, but here are the general characteristics of some of the most common hardwoods:

Poplar. This is often the least expensive of the hardwoods and also one of the softest, which makes it easy to work with. Poplar often exhibits wide grain with a greenish or yellowish tinge.

From left: poplar, hickory, red oak, and white oak.

Though it can be stained, poplar is often used for cabinetry that will be painted.

Hickory. Many people love hickory for its flamboyant beauty. Hickory has a wide grain and wide color variations, making individual boards memorably unique in appearance.

Hickory is usually expensive and is the heaviest and hardest of the hardwoods. It can be difficult to work with: It tends to split and/or produce tearout as you cut it. It reacts to changes in air humidity by swelling or shrinking, but this can be controlled if you finish it before building.

Red oak. This is one of the most abundant and least expensive of the hardwoods and has long been popular. Colors range from light tan to reddish or pinkish brown. It is often lightly stained to produce a "honey oak" appearance but can be stained darker for a much richer tone. It is medium-hard, easy to cut and fasten, and is reliably stable, effectively resisting warping and splitting.

Red oak has a coarse, pronounced grain as well as open pores. Expect to spend a good deal of time sanding before you apply finish. Gel stains often work best because they fill as they stain.

White oak. Less abundant and more expensive than red oak, white oak has colors that range from nearly white to fairly dark brown. It has more variation in grain patterns, which can be pronounced in some boards. Like red oak, it is hard but still easy to work with. It is less coarse grained than red oak, making it easier to stain to a variety of tones.

Alder. Most commonly available as red alder, this species is a relatively soft hardwood. Its sapwood can be light brown, but the heartwood is much darker, with red or yellow tinges, as seen in the top photo on the facing page. The grain is straight and uniform in texture. Alder is fairly easy to cut and fasten and can be stained to closely resemble walnut or cherry.

Walnut. Walnut is sometimes creamy white, but is best known for its dark browns, which range from chocolate to purplish in tone. Often the lighter sapwood is steamed to darken it. Grains vary from straight to very wavy, and some boards are stunningly curvy and swirling. Unfortunately, it can be very expensive.

Walnut is medium-hard and is easy to cut and fasten. It accepts stain readily and will remain stable and warp-free as long as it is dry when installed.

Maple. There are actually a number of maple subspecies with different characteristics. Hard maple is very light colored, with a smooth texture and wide grain. It is extremely hard, making it a challenge to cut and mill, and it can be quite expensive.

Soft maple has more variation in color and grain and it is also less expensive and easier to work with.

Figured maple comes in several different types and has something of a cult following among wood lovers. The most famous figures are bird's-eye maple, with a pattern of tiny, swirling dots that look a bit like eyes, and tiger maple, with stripes that run across the grain.

Cherry. Lots of people, including many woodworkers, are in love with cherry. It has a beautiful grain, with colors ranging from a very light sapwood to a much darker heartwood that exhibits subtle oranges or, well, cherry reds.

Cherry is very hard, but provided your blade is sharp, it is not difficult to cut and shape. It will stay stable and warp-free. Unfortunately, it is expensive.

WOOD GRAINS

Wood variations are further enhanced by the way the wood is cut from the tree, which determines the board's wood grain, as shown in "Anatomy of Wood" on p. 46. With some species—oak, for example—the visual difference between grain types is dramatic, while with others, such as cherry, the difference is less pronounced.

Boards with vertical grain are sometimes called quartersawn, and have straight grain lines that run close together. Flatsawn, or flat-grain boards have wavy patterns with a soft, arrowlike appearance. Many boards are somewhere between and can be called medium-grained.

From left: alder, walnut, maple, and cherry.

From left: flat grain, medium grain, and vertical grain.

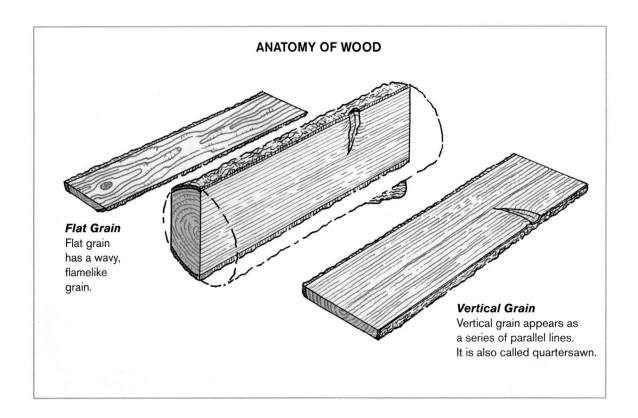

ANATOMY OF WOOD

Flat Grain
Flat grain has a wavy, flamelike grain.

Vertical Grain
Vertical grain appears as a series of parallel lines. It is also called quartersawn.

tip
If you have access to a sawmill, you can get great prices and have some fun looking through stacks of boards. However, the boards may not be graded, and you'll need to check each board closely for lumber defects and moisture content. If the boards are roughsawn, you'll need to spend plenty of time thickness planing, jointing, and sanding to prepare the boards for use.

The tighter and straighter the grain, the more stable the board; that's an important consideration when dealing with softwoods and boards used outdoors. But unless your hardwood boards are wider than 4 in. or are high in moisture content, the grain pattern is mostly a cosmetic issue.

BLEMISHES OR CHARACTER?

The next few pages show some common visual elements often found on boards. Some are definitely blemishes, some are definitely attractive features, and others may be one or the other, depending on your opinion. Interesting grain patterns are often generally referred to as "figuring."

LUMBER DEFECTS

- If a board exhibits **twist**, you may be able to use short pieces of it, but a pronounced twist is very difficult to straighten.

- A narrow board with a light **cup** can be surface-planed flat, but cupping is difficult to straighten in hardwoods.

- If a board has a slight **bow**, it can often be straightened during installation. Or you can use a jointer to plane a side of the board straight. A more pronounced bow, called a **crook**, usually cannot be straightened.

- If **end splits** are very short, they can be cut off. If a longer split is near the center of the board, you can rip-cut the board along the split line, resulting in two narrow boards that will be usable.

- **Surface checks** are usually a cosmetic problem, but one that probably cannot be sanded away.

- Boards that **wave** visibly along their faces are very difficult to straighten or plane smooth.

- You may be able to cut around **knots** or you may appreciate the look of small knots. If knots are large and porous, or even produce holes, the board is probably not worth buying.

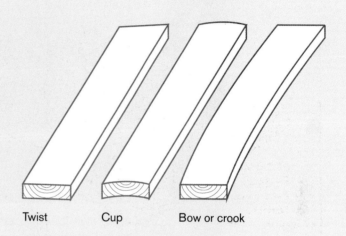

Twist   Cup   Bow or crook

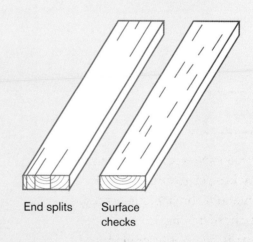

End splits   Surface checks

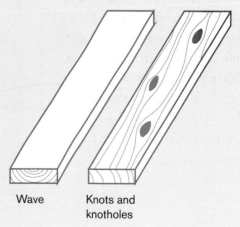

Wave   Knots and knotholes

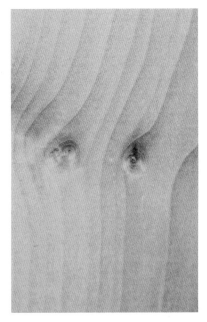

Burl is a darkened twist or swirl that is almost a knot—but not quite.

Quartersawn figuring. When wood—especially oak—is quartersawn, this type of figuring may result.

Wane is bark or the rounded place where bark used to be. It must be cut away.

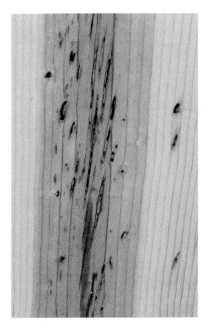

Grub holes. Whether caused by worms or not, these holes may be $1/16$ in. to $1/4$ in. wide, usually too deep to be sanded away.

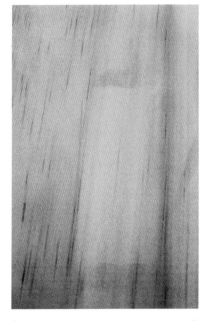

Sticker stain, caused by the small pieces of wood placed between drying wood, may be gray or brown, or lighter in color than the rest of the wood. A dark blemish may be difficult to stain away; for a light mark, stain or bleach the surrounding area to match.

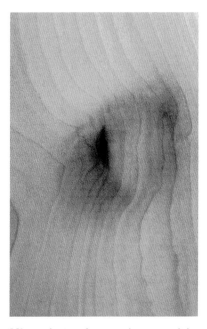

Mineral streaks may be greenish or charcoal in color. They may run along the grain or may be generally blotchy.

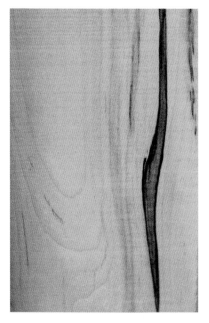

Pith is the soft core in the center of a tree.

A combination of dark heartwood and lighter-colored sapwood can be found in many boards.

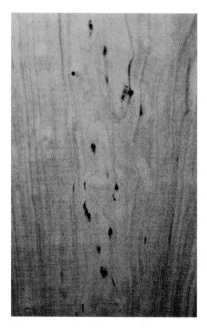

Gum streaks. Cherry boards with scattered gum streaks are often sought after for their beauty.

A milling error can create a rough spot where marks run sideways to the grain. Of course, the deeper the marks, the more sanding you will need to do.

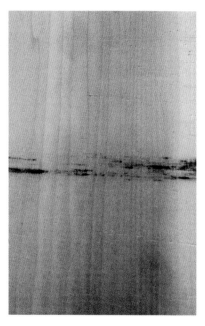

Transport marks. Wrapping boards with straps and transporting them can create dark stains and pockmarks in the boards. Check the other side of the board to see if it looks better.

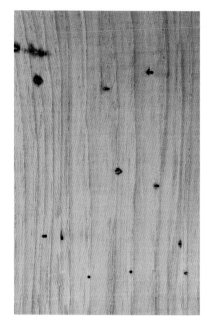

Peck holes. These may or may not be made by woodpeckers, and may or may not be considered attractive. They usually cannot be sanded away.

4 basic building methods

THE CHAPTERS that follow will show plenty of techniques and tips for building specific types of kitchen wall and base cabinets as well as bathroom vanities. This chapter gets you started with some fundamental methods for several of the most common procedures: cutting sheets and boards; edge-banding; rabbeting; and assembling with nails, screws, and pocket screws. These are methods you'll use over and over again.

You may already be well versed in many of these techniques, in which case you could skip this chapter and go on to the instructions for particular projects. But it doesn't hurt to brush up on the basics and you may find a new tip or two to help you save time and money.

Before you get going on a project, take the time to get organized so work will be more pleasure than pain. Stack your lumber and sheet goods so they will stay straight. Arrange your tools and fasteners so you can reach for them almost without thinking. And get your dust collection and cleaning products lined up, so you can move seamlessly from one tool to another without hassle. Work in an unhurried manner, double-checking measurements and thinking through the next few steps. That way, you can enjoy the process of making beautiful cabinets.

Measuring and Marking

A well-built project must start with cut lines that are precisely correct. Measuring and marking are not difficult, but it's easy to make mistakes. Work on developing good measuring and marking habits, so you won't have to recut or even throw out miscut pieces.

Measuring with a tape is often the only option. But wherever possible, measure by holding a board in place and marking it for the cut. When you cut multiple pieces to the same dimension, use the first board or sheet as a guide for marking and cutting the others, rather than using a tape measure for each cut.

1 To mark for a cut, hook the tape on one end of the board, pull taut, and draw a V shape, with its point at the exact dimension for the cut.

2 Hold your pencil tip on the point of the V, and slide a square over the board and against the pencil. Draw a line for the cut. To ensure that you will not cut the wrong side of the line, mark an X on the waste side.

tip

A tape measure's tip slides back and forth by about $1/8$ in., which is its thickness. This sliding ensures that your measurements will be the same whether you hook it onto the end of a board and pull or press it against a wall or other board for an inside measurement.

Cutting Sheet Goods

To make a number of cabinets, you'll want to cut sheets accurately and quickly. A tablesaw with a large table is the ideal tool, but surprisingly good results can be had with a circular saw as well.

CUTTING WITH A TABLESAW

If you are experienced at cutting sheet goods and have a large table that supports a full sheet throughout the cut—and perhaps a helper as well—you could simply make finish cuts with a single pass. However, even many professionals find that approach risky. It's easy for the large sheet to go off course, which can ruin the cut. So for most of us it's a good idea to first cut the sheet roughly and a bit larger than needed, and then make finish cuts with the resulting smaller pieces.

3 Many carpenters prefer to mark with a knife. This eliminates the need for erasing pencil lines and it helps keep the cut clean of tearout (as long as you consistently cut to the side of the line rather than through it).

1 Most factory edges are nice and straight, but some have waves and bumps that can make your cut go awry. Quickly check with a straightedge.

2 Rough-cut the sheet ½ in. or so larger than it needs to be. You can do this with a circular saw or the tablesaw. To ensure that you will not place the rough-cut side against the fence for the final cut (Step 3), draw a wavy line along it.

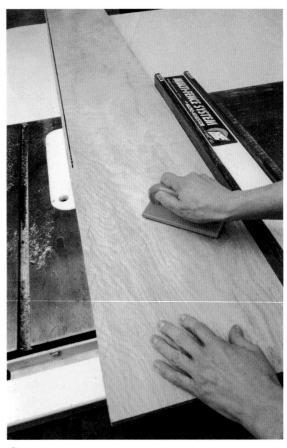

3 Make the final cut on your tablesaw. Use push tools to keep your hands away from the blade. If possible, push through the cut with one stroke; stopping and starting often creates unevenness in the cut.

tip

It can help to have someone hold the sheet at the other end, especially if you do not have outfeed support for a long cut. On the other hand, it can also hinder: If the helper pulls aggressively while you push, the sheet can move away from the fence, which will make the cut inaccurate. Have the helper gently support the other end of the sheet through most of the cut, and perhaps pull it only for the last 6 in. or so.

tip

If you have a small shop and handling full-size sheets will be difficult to manage, have the lumberyard or home center make the rough cuts for you. The cost is usually minimal.

MINIMIZING TEAROUT

It's vital that your sheet good cuts be smooth and free of tearout—the series of small splinters that sometimes occurs on the top side of the cut. Tearout occurs most often when you are making a crosscut (cutting across the grain), but it can also happen during rip cuts (cutting with the grain). When cutting melamine sheets, MDF, or particleboard, tearout is always a possibility.

Make some test cuts in scrap pieces before cutting the real thing. If you get tearout, here are some steps to take:

- Use a sharp blade that is recommended for your plywood or melamine. Adjust its height so the teeth rise only partway above the sheet; if the full teeth are above the sheet, tearout is more likely (A).

- Install a zero-clearance insert in the tablesaw (B). Typically, you will lower the blade below the table, attach the insert, turn on the saw, and slowly raise the blade to cut through the insert. As a result, the sheet will be supported tightly on each side as you cut, which reduces tearout.

- If you are cutting with a circular saw, you can make a zero-tolerance baseplate. Adjust the blade all the way up, so it doesn't protrude below the baseplate. Attach a piece of MDF to the baseplate by drilling countersunk holes and fastening with flat-head bolts. With the baseplate well supported, loosen the depth-adjusting nut, turn on the saw, and slowly lower the blade so it cuts through the MDF (C).

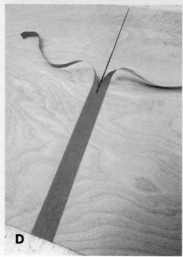

- Press a strip of painters' tape over the cut line and cut through it (D). This holds the wood fibers in place during the cut.

CUTTING WITH A CIRCULAR SAW

Some cabinetmakers would be horrified by the thought of cutting with a circular saw, but many cabinets have been made this way. Test your saw on scrap pieces to be sure it makes reliable cuts that do not waver; most mid- to upper-level circular saws will work.

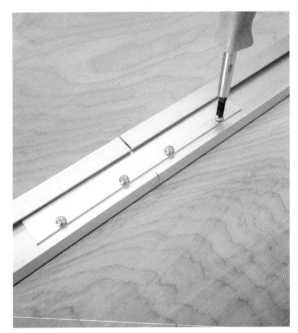

2 Use an inexpensive straightedge tool to ensure a straight long cut. This tool screws together to form an 8-ft.-long guide.

1 Measure the distance from the edge of the baseplate to the blade (above) and transfer this measurement to the board. Make one mark for the actual cut and another mark for the position of the guide (right).

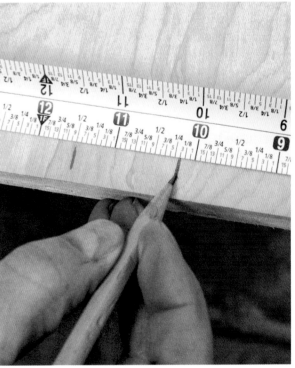

3 Support the sheet (as shown in "Other Circular Saw Guides" at right) so it will not fall away when you finish the cut. Position yourself so you can make the cut in one pass, without stopping and starting. With the baseplate pressed against the guide and held flat on the board, cut the sheet.

tip

Instead of measuring for the position of the cutting guide, you could first cut freehand along your cut line for an inch or so. Turn off the saw but leave it in position then slide the guide over to meet the baseplate and clamp it. Clamp the other end the same distance from the edge of the board.

OTHER CIRCULAR SAW GUIDES

Many carpenters produce reliable crosscuts using a Speed Square as a guide; the large square shown in the top photo below works better because it is easier to hold firmly in place as you cut. With a bit of practice you can also make straight rip cuts using a rip guide, as shown in the bottom photo below.

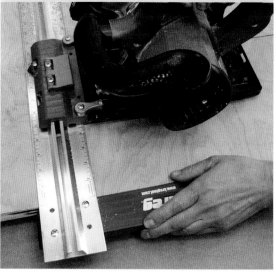

Crosscutting with a Miter Saw

Adjusted for accuracy and equipped with a sharp blade and an adjacent table, a miter saw is ready to make quick and accurate crosscuts with ease.

1 To make sure you cut accurately on the line, hold the board in place with the saw turned off. Lower the blade until its edge touches the cut line and adjust the position of the board as needed. Then raise the blade, turn on the saw, and make the cut.

2 To cut a series of boards all the same length, clamp a board to the fence to act as a stop.

CHOPSAW GUIDE

An aftermarket system like the one shown here is quicker and easier to use than a clamped-board guide. It includes a track with measuring tape and an adjustable stop. Once you've carefully set it up, it will be easy to measure for cuts without a tape measure and to cut a series of boards to exactly the same length.

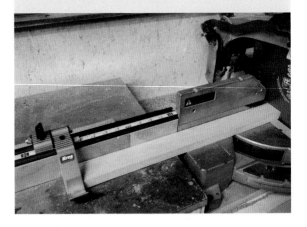

3 Here's a quick way to duplicate a cut: Place the board you want to duplicate on top of the board to be cut, with the ends flush. Guide the blade so it just grazes the top board and make the cut.

Edge-Banding

Edge-banding is the application of veneer along a visible edge of plywood. This is a critical skill for frameless cabinets because the front edges are very much on display. Applying iron-on banding is quick and easy, but it can be a challenge to get all the corners covered with crisp, clean lines. Even if you build face-frame cabinets, you may want to make the shelves out of plywood, in which case you will need to learn this skill.

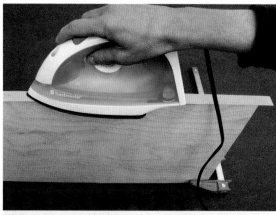

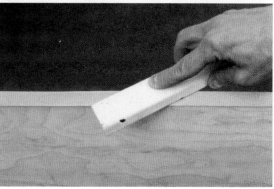

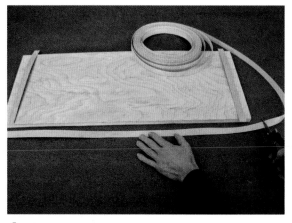

1 Cut the edge-banding pieces 1 in. or so longer than they need to be. You can cut with scissors, a knife, or a sharp chisel.

2 Heat up a household iron. Hold the strip in place, so it overlaps the sheet edge on both ends and on both sides. Press the iron onto the banding and keep it moving until the glue softens and adheres. Continue pressing for 5 to 10 seconds after the band is stuck. Remove the iron and press along the band with a smooth board to ensure a tight seal at all points.

tip

The iron should cause the band's glue to soften and bubble within a few seconds but should not be so hot as to burn the banding. Start with a setting between "cotton" and "polyester" and adjust as needed.

3 Cut the first piece of banding flush with the sheet ends. You can use a razor (as shown): Press down until you have cut most of the way through, then bend back to snap the band off. Or use scissors.

4 Use a small sanding block to lightly sand the edge of the first piece of banding, holding the block flat on the adjacent edge, until the banding's cut end is flush with the edge.

5 Apply banding to the other edge or edges in the same way and cut the ends nearly flush.

tip

Some pros use a sharp chisel or knife to cut off the edges. This takes practice.

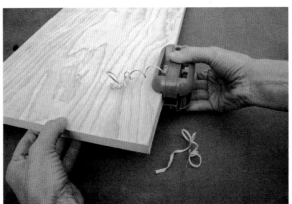

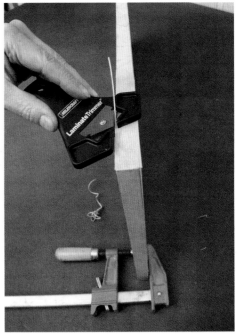

6 Trim the banding edges almost flush, so you can then sand them easily. Here I use two tools made for the purpose. The blue tool cuts through both sides at once and the black one cuts one side at a time. Use a tool that you are comfortable with.

Working with Melamine Sheets

Melamine sheets are a popular choice for cabinet-makers because they are inexpensive, they don't need to be sealed or painted, and they have a surface that is easy to wipe clean. But there are downsides: The surface—which may be white or colored or in a faux-wood pattern—lacks the warmth of natural wood, and once chipped or dented, melamine is difficult if not impossible to repair satisfactorily.

Melamine sheets can be cut and edge-banded or covered with a face frame in much the same way as plywood. However, there are some special techniques and considerations when working with melamine.

Cutting. Melamine is a bit easier to chip than plywood while cutting. And a cut with minor imperfections will not be easy to disguise with edge-banding. Be sure to use a fine-cutting blade with 80 or more teeth, for a clean-looking cut.

Fastening with screws. Melamine's particleboard core is easily split. If you drive a standard screw without first drilling a pilot hole, the sheets will likely crack open, resulting in ugly bulges and screws that do not hold. Practice fastening scrap pieces before driving screws into the real sheets to be sure your screws grab firmly without splitting the material.

Glue doesn't work when fastening a melamine surface. However, if you are attaching a wood face frame or if you are attaching particleboard to particleboard, then glue will hold well.

You may choose to first drive pilot holes, as shown in the photo at middle right. Use the correct size pilot screw or you may use special self-tapping screws (see the photo at bottom right). Some of these screws are designated as particleboard screws, while others are more general in purpose. (Note that in our example, one of the screws driven near the end of the particleboard created a slight split. It's a good idea to drill pilot holes near the ends, although screws in the middle can be driven without pilot holes.)

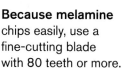

Because melamine chips easily, use a fine-cutting blade with 80 teeth or more.

When working with melamine it's a good idea to drive pilot holes. Use a pilot screw of just the right size—the thickness of the screw's shank, not including the threads (top). Or, you may use special self-tapping screws, which clear out the hole while you drive them (bottom).

Even when you use the right screws, they will not hold as well as screws driven into plywood. So use more of them and space them 4 in. to 6 in. apart.

Pocket screws. Pocket screws are often used with melamine. Like regular screws, they don't hold as firmly as screws driven into plywood, so use plenty of them (see the photo at left).

Drilling pocket-screw holes in particleboard often produces slight "mushrooms" in the edge of the sheet. Sand these smooth before you drive the screws.

Melamine edge-banding. Applying edge-banding on melamine is not particularly difficult, but minor flaws will be noticeable, so work carefully. See "Edge-Banding" on p. 57 for general techniques. The edge should be cleanly cut and perfectly straight. Apply the banding with an iron and cut the ends with a pair of scissors. (It's easier to cut than wood edge-banding.) You will likely end up with a very thin dark line at each edge; work to be sure this line is consistent in width. This is difficult to achieve using a regular knife or sanding block; special edge-banding cutters and sanders, as shown in the photo below, will produce more satisfying results.

You'll need to use plenty of pocket screws because, like regular screws, they won't hold as well with melamine. Sand any "mushrooms" (inset) away before you drive screws.

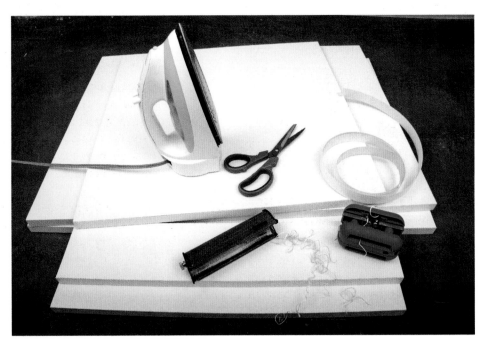

The techniques and tools needed for melamine edge-banding are very similar to those for wood edge-banding, but minor flaws will be more noticeable.

Jointing with a Router Table

Jointing straightens out rough board edges. It also planes edges perfectly straight in preparation for gluing up side by side. If you do not have a jointer (see p. 28), you can do the job with a tablesaw (see pp. 146–148), or use a router table with a two-part adjustable fence, as shown here.

1 Loosen the hold-down screws on the left side of the router table's adjustable fence (the side you will push the board toward while routing). Adjust it outward by 1/32 in. or 1/16 in. On this table, special rods are inserted to make the adjustment. Tighten the screws. This adjustment will cause the router to cut a bit of the edge and support the cut edge as it is fed through.

2 Put a straight-cutting bit on the router. Adjust the fence so the router bit is flush with the fence you adjusted in Step 1 and position the guard. When you push the board through, a small amount will be planed off the edge. Repeat if needed to fully straighten the board.

Cutting Dadoes and Rabbets

A dado is a groove in the middle of a board; a rabbet is a groove along its edge. To make either, you can use a tablesaw or a router table.

If using a tablesaw, start by assembling dado blades with a total width that is the thickness of the desired dado and adjust the blade height for the desired depth. If you have a 1/4-in.-wide dado to cut, you may choose to do it with two passes using a standard blade.

1 Clamp a board to the side of the tablesaw's fence so you do not cut into the fence's metal, adjust it so the dado blades are nearly touching the clamped board, and cut the rabbet (or position the fence the correct distance away and cut the dado).

If you want to rout a dado, a router table is recommended; it's easy to go astray when routing with a rip guide. Adjust a straight bit of the desired width to the correct height for the dado depth and make the cut on the router table.

Attaching with Nails and Screws

Fastener heads should never be visible on finished and installed cabinets. Sinking nails or screws and filling the holes with wood filler is acceptable when attaching moldings in a room but not for cabinetry. (The exception is pin nails, which are virtually invisible, but they do not hold well and are used to hold boards still while the glue, which provides all the joint's strength, dries.) So pocket screws, biscuits, or dowels are used to attach visible elements. However, much of a cabinet will be hidden once assembled and then covered by a countertop; therefore, many joints are fastened with nails or screws, often with the assistance of wood glue.

You can use a router with a self-guided rabbet bit for rabbets, as shown.

1 It sometimes helps to fasten a square-cut piece of plywood (with two factory edges) temporarily onto your workbench or floor so you can press boards against it as you work. This allows you to press firmly without fear that the boards will go out of square.

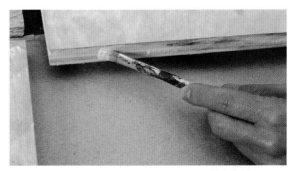

2 When working with wood, glue is a great fastening aid, though it cannot be relied on to work alone. Once you have determined where two pieces will be attached, apply wood glue to one or both edges or sides. Swipe with a brush, a board, or your finger to maintain a fairly even layer of glue, so it will adhere at all points and will not squeeze out in globs.

3 Drive 1¼-in. finish nails to hold the pieces together temporarily until you drive screws or 2-in. or 2½-in. nails to fasten permanently. The problem with longer nails is that they sometimes curve while being driven and then poke out of the sides. So drive them at a slight angle toward the nonvisible side.

4 Opinions vary on when to scrape or wash away glue squeeze-out. Many woodworkers believe it's best to allow the glue to start to harden, but not harden completely, and then scrape most of it away. Allow the rest to harden and sand smooth.

tip

If the finish nails in Step 3 poke out, remove them by grabbing their pointed ends with a pair of end nippers, then roll the nippers to pull them through.

5 Pilot holes not only keep boards from splitting but actually strengthen the screw's fastening ability. The pilot bit should be about the width of the fastener minus the threads. Drill a pilot hole with a bit that also cuts a counterbore—a shallow convex hole that allows the screw's head to sit flat (left). (Without counterboring, screwing will raise up little splinters that make cabinet installation difficult.) Then drive the screws (right).

6 You can often skip drilling pilot holes if you use trimhead screws (left), which sink into most materials without raising a bump. For stronger fastening, use self-tapping screws (right), which create pilot and countersink holes as they are driven.

Pocket Screws

In recent years, pocket screws have taken the cabinetry world by storm. You'll see them in use throughout this book because they fasten boards or sheets together—most often at a 90° angle, but also end to end—quickly and firmly. The downside is that they make long visible holes on one side of the joint. In most cases, you can position these holes so they will not be visible once the cabinet is in place. Or you can cover the holes with special caps or plugs. You can use pocket screws to fasten hardwood, plywood, MDF, or melamine sheets.

tip
Manufacturers say that glue is not needed when fastening with pocket screws, but many cabinetmakers apply glue for extra strength.

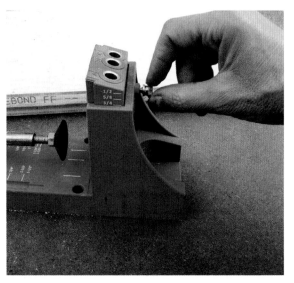

1 There are various types of pocket-screw jigs, but here I use one of the most common. You may choose to fasten the jig to your workbench. Then set the jig's guide for the thickness of stock you will fasten—usually ³⁄₄ in. for the cabinets and ¹⁄₂ in. for the drawer bodies.

2 Use the drill bit specified for the screws you will drive. Set the bit in the gauge, position the collar for the thickness of the board, and tighten the collar.

3 Clamp the sheet to be fastened in the jig and drill a hole until the bit's collar meets the jig. On sheet goods, drill holes every 6 in. to 8 in. You need to drill holes in only this sheet or board; the self-tapping screws will drive into the other board without splitting.

4 Use screws of the correct length: 1¼-in. screws for ¾-in. stock and 1-in. screws for ½-in. stock. Use fine-thread screws when driving into hardwood and coarse-thread screws for driving into plywood or melamine. Clamp the board to be fastened firmly to the work surface or to the board being fastened; various clamps are suited to different situations. Clamping keeps the board from wandering while you drive the screw. Drive the screws to fasten.

5 When fastening narrow pieces, like those of a face frame, use at least two screws to keep the boards from twisting.

5 face frames

EVEN THOUGH a cabinet's face frame will be nearly invisible until the doors or drawers are opened, many people prefer the look and feel of cabinets with face frames because they cover the edges of plywood or melamine more durably than the edge-banding used for frameless cabinets.

Face frames also provide a kind of security when building: Though some cabinetmakers build the cases first, it's safer to build the face frames first. Once all the frames are made and measured and you are certain they will fit in the kitchen, you can cut the sheet goods and build the cabinet cases with confidence. Further, the traditional 1/4-in. face-frame overlap on the sides makes it easier to deal with wavy and out-of-square walls when installing.

If you plan to build frameless cabinets, you can completely skip this chapter and go on to the instructions in the next two chapters for building cabinets.

Planning Face Frames

The cabinet case will typically be 1/2 in. narrower than the frame. But the frame determines the actual installation width of the cabinet—how much space it takes up on the wall.

The projects in this book generally feature face frames made of 1×2s: 3/4 in. thick and 1 1/2 in. wide. This size works well if you install doors and drawer faces that nearly cover the frame. If you want more of the frame to show for a more traditional look, you may choose to use 2-in. or wider pieces; however, keep in mind that wider frame pieces will slightly restrict access into the cabinets and will make the drawers narrower.

Draw a plan for your project carefully on graph paper or use a design program (see p. 7). From the drawing you can produce a cut list for all your frame pieces.

OVERLAYS

If you build with face frames, the most common arrangement is to use 1 1/2-in.-wide pieces for the rails and stiles, positioning the stiles (the vertical pieces) so they overlap the outside of the cabinet sides by 1/4 in. Assuming you build with 3/4-in. plywood, the stiles will overlap the inside of the cabinet by 1/2 in. Of course, if you choose wider stiles, the dimensions will be different. And at the end of a row of cabinets, you may choose to install the last rail flush with the outside edge of the case.

DIMENSIONS

Wall cabinet face frames are simple to dimension: They are exactly the desired width and height of the cabinet. (As I said earlier, the cabinet case itself will be 1/2 in. narrower than the total cabinet size because the frame most often overhangs by 1/4 in. on each side.)

HINGES FOR DIFFERENT OVERLAYS

Choose hinges that match your inner face-frame overlays. If you are building frameless cabinets, buy hinges that will allow the doors to cover the cabinet edges fully or partially, according to your preference.

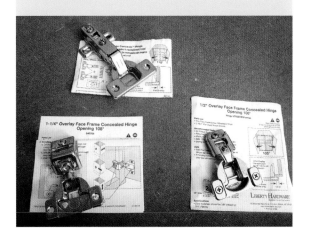

FACE FRAME FOR INSET DOORS

If you plan to install inset doors or doors that only partially overlay the frame, you may choose to build with narrower stiles where two cabinets meet in order to keep the distance between doors consistent.

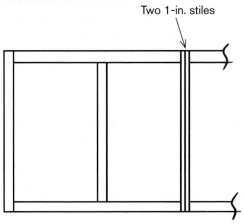

Two 1-in. stiles

Most rails and stiles are 2 in. wide.

FACE-FRAME OVERLAYS

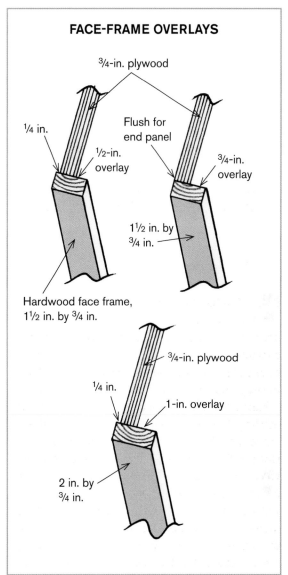

¾-in. plywood

¼ in.

Flush for end panel

½-in. overlay

¾-in. overlay

1½ in. by ¾ in.

Hardwood face frame, 1½ in. by ¾ in.

¾-in. plywood

¼ in.

1-in. overlay

2 in. by ¾ in.

tip

If you plan to install crown molding on top of your wall cabinets, you may need to install a wider top rail to provide a nailing surface. Determine this before you build the frames.

FACE-FRAME PLAN FOR WALL CABINETS

In a standard installation, where the doors will nearly cover the face frame when they are closed, you simply build all the cabinets with stiles and rails in the same thickness. An exception: Here the stile along the wall is ½ in. wider. This provides more room for opening the door (if the hinge is next to the wall) and allows room for a scribe cut, if the wall is not straight or plumb.

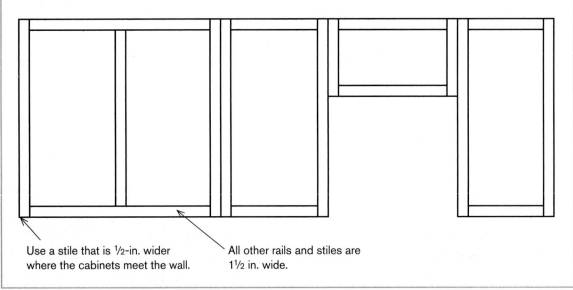

Use a stile that is ½-in. wider where the cabinets meet the wall.

All other rails and stiles are 1½ in. wide.

FACE FRAME FOR BASE CABINETS

Here are the three most common types of base cabinets configurations. You can, of course, adjust the sizes—say, if you want a taller drawer for some large items.

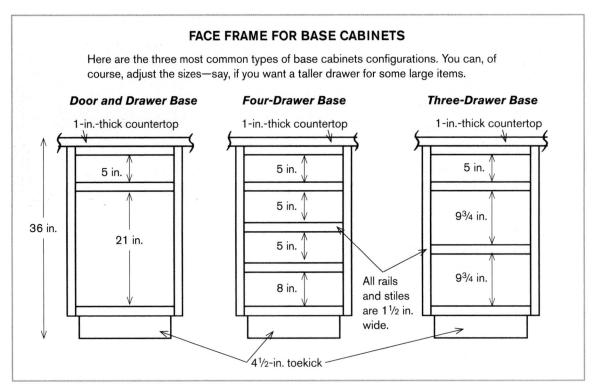

Door and Drawer Base

1-in.-thick countertop

5 in.

21 in.

36 in.

Four-Drawer Base

1-in.-thick countertop

5 in.

5 in.

5 in.

8 in.

Three-Drawer Base

1-in.-thick countertop

5 in.

9¾ in.

9¾ in.

All rails and stiles are 1½ in. wide.

4½-in. toekick

Base cabinet frames are the desired width of the cabinet, but the height depends on two factors: the height of the toekick and the thickness of the countertop. Most people will want the countertop to be 36 in. high. In the example shown in "Face Frame for Base Cabinets" on the facing page, the toekick is 4½ in. high and the countertop will be 1 in. thick. If you want a shorter toekick (some are only 3½ in.) or if your countertop is thinner or thicker (they vary from ¾ in. to 1½ in.), then adjust your dimensions accordingly.

tips

Some tall slide-out trash or recycle containers call for a base cabinet that has only a door and no top drawer (see p. 177). Be sure to read the manufacturer's instructions before you make the cabinet.

Most commonly, a face frame's bottom rail is installed with its top edge flush with, or $1/16$ in. lower than, the case's bottom shelf for easy cleaning and sliding of items. The top of the top rail is usually flush with the top of the case, and the vertical stiles overlap the outside of the cabinet case by $1/4$ in.

Decide at this point what you will use for the base underneath the cabinet and whether you will have the face frame underhang the cabinet. For more, see p. 114.

Cutting and Preparing Frame Pieces

Precision is key to successful face-frame construction. If the overall widths are even $1/32$ in. off, the mistake will multiply as you build additional frames and could result in frames that do not fit or that are out of square. Work with care and use simple jigs wherever possible to ensure multiple cuts that are uniform in size.

Gang-cut your face-frame pieces. Make sure that there is at least one good edge for each piece because the inside edge will be exposed at all times.

Often the face frame is made from the same species of wood as the cabinet's plywood—but not always. You may choose, for instance, to make the case out of wood-look melamine and the frame out of hardwood. If the cabinet will be painted, birch plywood with a poplar face frame is a sensible choice.

Aim to produce finished pieces that are precisely $1^1/_2$ in. wide (or whatever width you choose). However, if you are off by $^1/_{16}$ in. it will not be apparent, as long as you measure for the rails using the method shown in the photo below.

RIP-CUTTING THE PIECES

You may be able to purchase ready-cut S4S (smooth on four sides) pieces of 1×2 in the hardwood of your choice. Often, however, you can save money by buying wider boards and rip-cutting them to width.

If you will be using a jointer, rip the boards $^1/_{16}$ in. to $^1/_8$ in. wider than the desired width. The jointer will remove about that much material. If you plan to use a sander, rip the boards $^1/_{32}$ in. or $^1/_{16}$ in. wider.

Use a blade that produces a fairly smooth surface without wearing down quickly. For hardwoods, a rip-cutting blade will last longer than a finish blade. The cut edge of the face frame boards will be visible, so there may be a trade-off: A long-lasting blade may produce a fairly rough cut, which you will need to sand.

MEASURING AND CUTTING TO LENGTH

Cut the (vertical) stiles all to the desired height of the cabinets. Use a stop guide to duplicate the cuts (see p. 56).

To measure for the rails, you can subtract 3 in. from the total width of the frame. But because

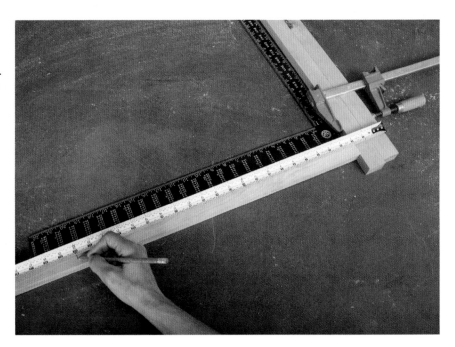

Measure and cut the rails carefully because they, along with the width of the stiles, determine the overall width of the cabinet.

tip

Some of the ripped pieces you cut will be wonderfully flat, straight, and free of imperfections on at least one side; others will have minor problems. Cut the longest pieces out of the really straight stuff. Many of the shorter pieces can be cut out of the stock that has minor bows and even twists.

board widths may vary slightly, a better way is to clamp two stiles together, press the rail against them, and measure for the rail length as shown in the photo on the facing page.

SANDING AND FINISHING

If you have a jointer or thickness planer, use it to smooth the cut edges (see p. 56). If not, work carefully with a random-orbit sander. Hold the sanding pad flat on the surface, so you don't round over the edges. You may choose to very slightly ease the edges with a hand sander so they aren't sharp, but don't round them over visibly.

Pocket-Screw Face Frame

With pocket screws you can make strong and square face frames quickly. See "Pocket Screws" on pp. 64–65 for more information.

tip

When fastening $3/4$-in. hardwood, use $1^{1}/4$-in. fine-thread pocket screws.

Hold a random-orbit sander flat on the boards as you sand. There is no need to press down hard; light to medium pressure is best.

1 The pocket screws will be driven in the back of the frame. Place the frame upside-down and mark to indicate where the screw holes will be drilled, so you don't get confused as you work.

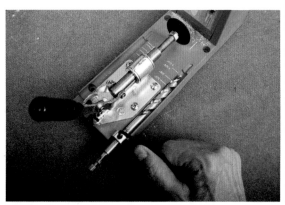

2 Use the pocket-screw jig's gauge to measure for the correct depth of the holes you will drill and tighten the collar. Drill two holes in the end of the backs of the rails.

3 Use a clamp made for pocket screws to hold a rail tightly against a stile and feel with your finger to be sure they are perfectly aligned. Use a framing square to keep the pieces at a right angle. You may choose to apply a small amount of glue to the joint before driving the screws. Drive the screws.

tip

If the stile moves slightly out of alignment when you drive the first screw, remove the screw, drill a new hole, and start again.

4 To check for square, measure the diagonals; they should be exactly the same distance.

tip

If a frame is very slightly out of square, you may be able to straighten it by holding it upright with just one corner resting on the work table and tapping with a hammer on the opposite corner. If this does not solve the problem, disassemble, drill new holes, and try again.

Screw-and-Plug Face Frame

The method outlined here produces visible plugs in the corners of the frame for a pleasant hand-crafted look, at the same time achieving very strong joints.

2 On a scrap piece of face-frame wood, drill multiple holes with the plug-cutting bit, then use a small chisel to pry out the plugs.

1 You'll need to buy a plug-cutting drill bit as well as a bit that drills both a pilot hole and a counterbore (not a countersink) hole. The plug cutter must make plugs of the same size as the counterbore—in this example, $5/16$ in. You'll also need a #1 square-drive bit and some square-drive trim-head screws. (In this setup, the pilot/counterbore bit can be quickly flipped for driving square-head screws.)

3 On the end of the stile, use a square to mark for two holes that are centered on the stile's thickness and evenly spaced.

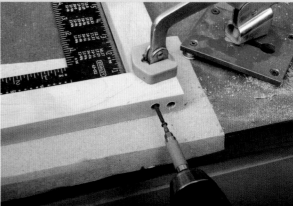

4 Clamp the pieces tightly together and check that they are square to each other. Using a small square as a general guide, drill a pilot hole about ½ in. deeper than the length of the screw, then drill a counterbore hole with a depth of at least ¼ in. Separate the pieces, apply a bit of glue to the joint, then reclamp and drive a trim-head screw into each hole until the joint tightens.

6 Allow the glue to dry completely. Use a hand sander or a random-orbit sander to sand the plugs flush.

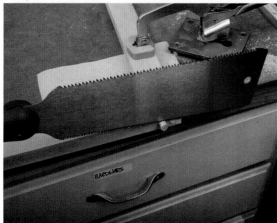

5 Squirt a dab of glue into the holes or onto the plugs and tap them in. After the glue dries, use a fine saw to cut the plugs close to flush.

Hidden-Dowel
Face Frame

Using dowels with glue is an old-fashioned method still popular with many woodworkers for attaching boards together invisibly and with no hardware. You can buy a self-centering dowel jig, but simply using centering pins is not difficult—and can be done quickly.

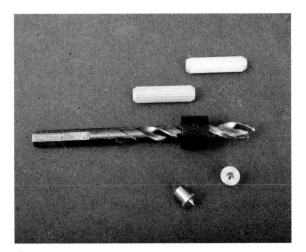

1 You'll need wood dowels (here I am using ⁵⁄₁₆ in., but you can also use ³⁄₈ in.), a drill bit the same size as the dowels, and dowel centers, also the same size. The wood dowels are fluted, to allow for plenty of glue to seep in and hold firmly.

2 Drill two holes into each joint. If you have a drill press, by all means use it. Or you may choose to use a portable drill press attachment (top). But the holes do not have to be precisely square; using a Speed Square as a general guide (above) works fine for someone with reasonable carpentry skills.

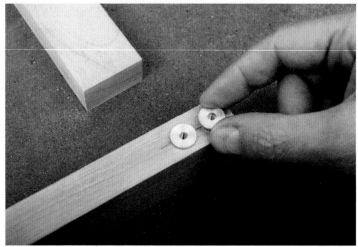

3 Clean out the holes with a knife, then insert a center into each hole.

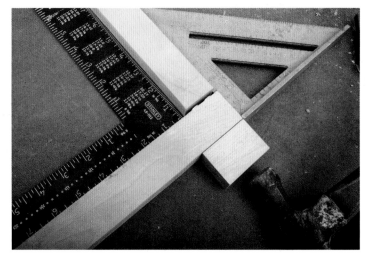

4 Position the boards as they will be attached and use a straightedge to be sure the rail is aligned with the stile. Position a small block as shown to prevent marring the wood as you tap. Holding the rail firm, tap the stile with medium pressure, so the centers make clearly visible indentations.

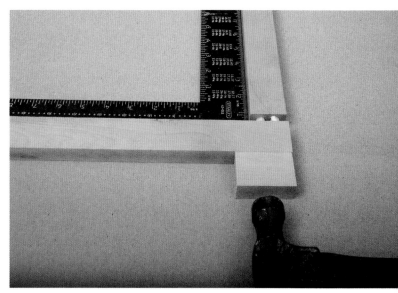

5 Insert the tip of the drill bit into one of the indentations made in the last step, drill, and then repeat for the second hole. Clean the holes out with a knife, so no fragments can get in the way of a tight joint.

6 Place a sheet of construction paper under the frame to catch squeezed-out glue. At each joint, squirt some glue into each hole, insert the dowel, and tap the pieces together.

tips

Use a brad-point bit when drilling the holes. It has a tip that easily inserts into the indentation made by the dowel center.

Have all your pieces ready before you start gluing and tapping the joints, so you can work quickly once you start. Otherwise, the glue will start to set up in the first joint by the time you get to the last joint.

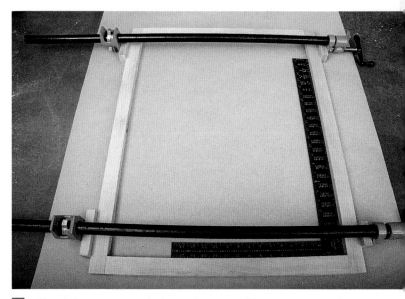

7 Check for square and clamp the assembly together. Allow at least 1 hour for the glue to dry before removing the clamps. After you remove the clamps, handle the frame carefully and let it dry overnight before attaching it to the cabinet.

Making a Beaded Face Frame

A bead detail adds elegance to a face frame. It's often applied when doors will be inset (so that the face frame is visible when doors and drawers are closed). There's nothing complicated about making and installing a single bead, but the work should be done precisely for a neat, professional appearance.

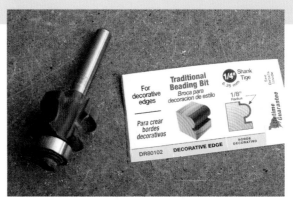

There are a number of beading bits available. Use one like this, which is called a "traditional beading bit."

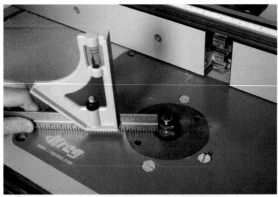

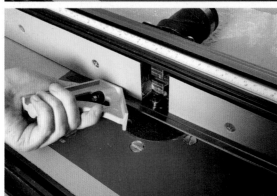

1 Here, I am using a beading bit with a ¼-in. radius, but you may choose a ³⁄₁₆-in. radius for a more pronounced look. Set the beading bit on a router table so the bottom of the bead is at the same height as the table. Set the router fence so the router will cut the bit's full thickness.

2 Rout a bead along one side of a piece of 1 × 2; then rout the other side. Set a tablesaw to rip-cut at ¼ in. and rip each side of the 1 × 2 to produce two bead pieces.

Adding a bead will, of course, widen the face-frame pieces, so be sure to take the extra width into account when planning. You may, for instance, choose to use $1^{1}/_{4}$-in.-wide boards for the basic frame with a $^{1}/_{4}$-in.-thick bead piece, for a total frame width of $1^{1}/_{2}$ in. If you add $^{1}/_{4}$-in. beading to a standard 1×2 frame, the total frame will be $1^{3}/_{4}$ in. wide—and you'll have a nice old-fashioned look without protruding too much into the cabinet cavity.

4 Hold the bead piece in place and use a knife to mark where you will miter-cut to length. Incise the mark on the bottom, where the tip of the miter will be.

3 Miter-cut one end of each bead piece. Make the miter cuts using a tablesaw with an angle gauge. Or use a power miter saw. Fit the miter saw with a wood fence; this makes it easier to get an exact cut on a narrow piece.

5 Test-fit the pieces and recut as needed for a snug (but not too tight) fit all round. Squirt a small amount of glue on the inside of the frame, align the bead piece, and drive a few pin nails to attach.

6 wall cabinets

WHEN TALKING with cabinetmakers about building kitchen cabinet cases, you will likely hear the phrase "more than one way to skin a cat." It's not clear why anyone would actually want to skin a cat, but the message is clear. Most kitchen cabinets are pretty simple boxes that have front edges built for attaching doors and a grid of holes inside for installing adjustable shelving. (The exception: corner cabinets get a bit complex.) Because they are simple, there are many ways to build them. This book emphasizes certain methods that I believe are strong and not difficult to build, but it also touches on other options.

With the exception of corner units, face-frame and frameless cabinets are built in much the same way; the main difference is whether you will attach a face frame or cover exposed edges with edge-banding. If you choose to go with face-frame cabinets, see chapter 5.

Some professional cabinetmakers build doors and drawer faces first, then the cases. You can proceed that way, but for many it's simpler and safer to build the cases first. Once you're sure the cases will fit in the space allotted, you can measure the cases to determine final door and drawer face sizes. This book also shows building wall cabinets first, then base cabinets (see chapter 7), but you may prefer to build the base cabinets first.

In a typical row of cabinets, only the outside of one cabinet will be visible. So once installed, most of the cabinet cases will be visible only when you open the door to see inside. I'll show you how to build so no fastener heads are showing on the one visible cabinet, but you may choose instead to cover the exposed side with a panel.

Getting Ready

To avoid heartbreaking mistakes, get all your ducks in a row before you start building the first cabinet case:

- Plan the kitchen carefully, so you know the exact size of every cabinet (see chapter 1).

- Check walls for square and plumb and allow for extra space if you need to add filler pieces to compensate for imperfections.

- Be sure all the doors will open fully, especially at the corners and where cabinets meet walls or appliances. You may need to add filler pieces between cabinets or between a cabinet and a wall.

- Buy your cabinet hinges ahead of time and be sure they will work with your cabinets.

- Choose materials and plan the finishing. If you are using natural-wood plywood or wood face frames, you may want to apply finish to pieces before assembling. You can also purchase plywood that is prefinished or decide to apply a finish after the cabinets are built (see chapter 9).

ASSEMBLY TABLE

When building cabinets, a workbench is often too high and working on the floor is often awkward—even painful after a while. A 16-in.-tall assembly table is just the right height for comfortable cabinet assembly. And if the table is on wheels, you can easily rotate your work, which you'll find a serious convenience.

Building an assembly table is well worth the hour or so of labor and the modest material cost. You'll need a single sheet of ¾-in. plywood, some short 2×4s, and four casters. The table shown is 40 in. by 30 in., which will support almost any kitchen cabinet. Buy plywood that is flat and free of warps. Cut the three 12-in.-wide joists carefully with a tablesaw so they are perfectly straight, to produce a table that is perfectly flat.

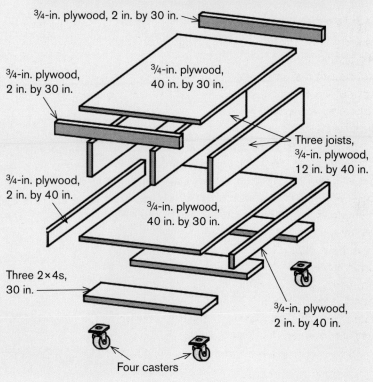

¾-in. plywood, 2 in. by 30 in.

¾-in. plywood, 2 in. by 30 in.

¾-in. plywood, 40 in. by 30 in.

Three joists, ¾-in. plywood, 12 in. by 40 in.

¾-in. plywood, 2 in. by 40 in.

¾-in. plywood, 40 in. by 30 in.

¾-in. plywood, 2 in. by 40 in.

Three 2×4s, 30 in.

Four casters

tip

In some areas it is not unusual to build with ⅝-in. rather than ¾-in. plywood. If you go this route, be sure to take the difference in thickness into account as you plan and build the cabinets. For instance, for the cabinets shown on p. 83, the horizontal pieces will need to be ¼ in. longer if you build with ⅝-in. plywood but the vertical pieces will be the same size.

Basic Wall Cabinet Construction

Whichever design you choose, everything must be straight and square; minor flaws may not be noticeable in a single cabinet, but when you join a number of cabinets in a row, the mistakes can multiply. So work carefully, following the cutting and joining techniques in chapter 4.

WALL CABINET DEPTH

Many wall cabinets have cases that are 12 in. deep, including the face frame if there is one. Once an overlaid door is added, the total depth is 12¾ in. However, there are other options:

- If you are building frameless cabinets using plywood, you may want to make them 11¾ in. deep. This will save on material costs because you can rip-cut four widths from a single 4-ft.-wide plywood sheet. (Remember that a sawcut is about ⅛ in. thick, so you cannot get four 12-in.-wide pieces out of a single sheet.) However, melamine sheets are typically 49 in. wide, making it possible to get four 12-in.-wide pieces out of a sheet.

- Many inexpensive cabinets are a total of 12 in. deep, including the door thickness—for a total case depth (including the face frame, if any) of only 11¼ in. This may, with very careful planning, save on material costs but can also feel a bit chintzy.

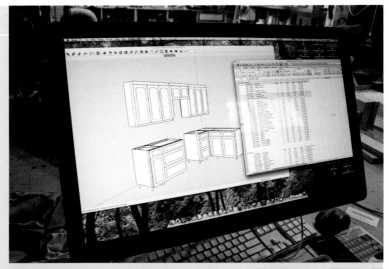

DESIGN SOFTWARE

Using SketchUp or another cabinet-design program, you can digitally build cabinets to the exact sizes you want. Such programs can then spit out a list of all the pieces you will need, with correct measurements for each one. With this information, you can cut a bunch of boards and mark them with reference numbers for assembly. The time spent learning such software can save a good deal more time down the line.

tip

Since most cabinet sides are not visible once installed, you can simply drive screws through the sides in most instances. However, if a side will be visible and you do not plan to attach a side panel later, common practice is to fasten with pocket screws on that side.

- Some cabinets are extra-deep—often 13 in. or 14 in., not including the door. This creates more storage room inside. However, a wall cabinet deeper than 14 in. may protrude too far from the wall, making it uncomfortable for someone working at a standard 25-in.-deep countertop.

Our Design

The drawings at right show frameless and face-frame wall cabinets, both of which we will build in this chapter. These cabinets feature a ¼-in. plywood back that is set in dadoes cut in the side pieces. This dado construction makes for a rock-solid cabinet that is sure not to pull apart even if the shelves are laden with heavy cans. (For that matter, even if children crawl on top, though that is not recommended.) Plywood cleats at the top and bottom of the back provide a strong surface for driving screws when attaching the cabinet to the wall.

tip

The designs shown at right are especially recommended if you will be building with melamine sheets because screws driven into melamine do not hold as well as those driven into plywood.

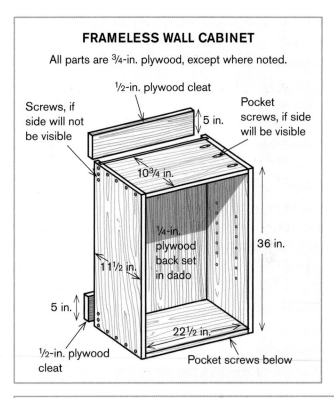

FRAMELESS WALL CABINET

All parts are ¾-in. plywood, except where noted.

½-in. plywood cleat

Screws, if side will not be visible

Pocket screws, if side will be visible

5 in.

10¾ in.

¼-in. plywood back set in dado

11½ in.

36 in.

5 in.

22½ in.

½-in. plywood cleat

Pocket screws below

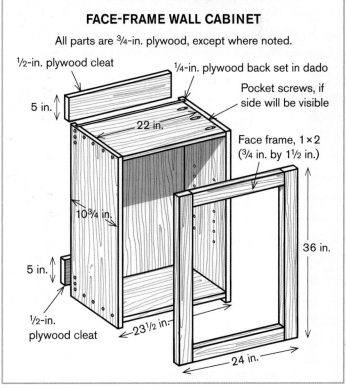

FACE-FRAME WALL CABINET

All parts are ¾-in. plywood, except where noted.

½-in. plywood cleat

¼-in. plywood back set in dado

Pocket screws, if side will be visible

5 in.

22 in.

Face frame, 1 × 2 (¾ in. by 1½ in.)

10¾ in.

36 in.

5 in.

½-in. plywood cleat

23½ in.

24 in.

Using ¼-in. plywood for the back saves a good deal of material expense because the back makes up a major portion of the material used. The top and bottom cleats can be made of inexpensive softwood plywood.

OTHER POSSIBILITIES

Two alternative designs are a bit simpler to build; they're strong, though not quite as strong as our preferred design. In "Wall Cabinet Design 2" below, a ¼-in. plywood back is screwed or nailed onto the sides, and ¾-in. plywood cleats are attached to the inside of the cabinet at the top and bottom. Where a side will show after installation, the side piece is cut ¼ in. longer than the other side, and a rabbet is cut to accept the plywood.

"Wall Cabinet Design 3" below shows the simplest design—a straightforward box made completely of ¾-in. plywood. Here, if a side will show, it should be attached with pocket screws driven from the back of the cabinet.

tip

A common shorthand way of referring to wall cabinets starts with the letter *W*, followed by the width, then the height. So, for instance, W2436 refers to a wall cabinet that's 24 in. wide and 36 in. tall. *CW* means a corner wall cabinet.

WALL CABINET DESIGN 2

¼-in. plywood back

¾-in. plywood cleat, 4 in. wide

¾-in. plywood cleat, 4 in. wide

If Side Will Show

Rabbet to accept ¼-in. plywood

¼-in. back

¾-in. plywood cleat

¾-in. plywood side

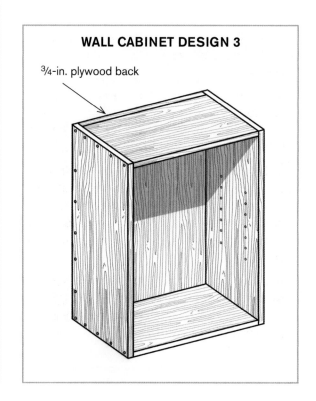

WALL CABINET DESIGN 3

¾-in. plywood back

Planning the Cuts

Wall cabinet part sizes are straightforward and easy to calculate. But it is notoriously easy to make simple arithmetic mistakes, which can result in a heavy cost in time and materials.

So it's an excellent idea to write up cut lists, which force you to double-check your figures so you don't cut any pieces too long or too short and so you don't cut more pieces of a certain size than you need. Cut charts are also very helpful; these are simple drawings that show how the pieces will be cut out of sheets. This will help you get the most out of a sheet, and save you money.

Here are some basic cut-list principles for wall cabinets:

- Except for corner cabinets, wall cabinet sides are all the same depth. In this design, frameless cabinets are 11½ in. deep and face-frame cabinets are 10¾ in. (Adding the face frame will make them a total of about 11½ in. deep.)

- Most of your cabinets will be the same height. So all the side pieces for your wall cabinets will be the same height, with the exception of pantry units and over-the-stove and refrigerator cabinets.

- In this design, all horizontal pieces, both tops and bottoms, are ¾ in. narrower than the side pieces to make room for the ½-in. plywood cleats and the dado with inset ¼-in. plywood back.

- In the frameless cabinets, the tops and bottoms are 1½ in. narrower than the total width of the cabinet. For a face-frame cabinet, they are 2 in. narrower than the total width (because the face frame overlays the cabinet by ¼ in. on each side).

- Assuming you are using shelf pins that do not limit the length of the shelves (see p. 90), the shelves will be ⅛ in. shorter than the top and bottom pieces.

tip

Melamine sheets are typically 49 in. by 97 in., giving you a bit more room to work.

MAKING A CUT CHART

Though it may seem tedious, you'll save money and minimize mistakes if you make a cut list and plan how the pieces can most efficiently be cut from sheets.

"Cut List for Two Cabinets, W2436 and W3036" on p. 86 shows a plan for cutting the parts for two cabinets out of a single sheet of plywood. This produces a very small amount of waste; for other cabinet sizes you may find that you have to throw away more scrap.

As you plan, pay attention to the direction of the wood grain. It's generally considered most attractive to run cabinet grain vertically rather than horizontally and for shelf grain to run lengthwise. This means that for wall cabinets you will probably start by rip-cutting pieces that are a bit narrower than 12 in. Of course, with white or solid-color melamine sheets you don't have to worry about this.

Building a Basic Wall Cabinet

Whether you're building a case for a standard face-frame or for a frameless wall cabinet, it is largely the same process. Besides the ¾-in. difference in cabinet depth, the main distinction is that with a face-frame cabinet you build the entire case and

tip

You'll probably produce a good deal of waste when cutting plywood backs, largely because you need to keep the grain running vertically.

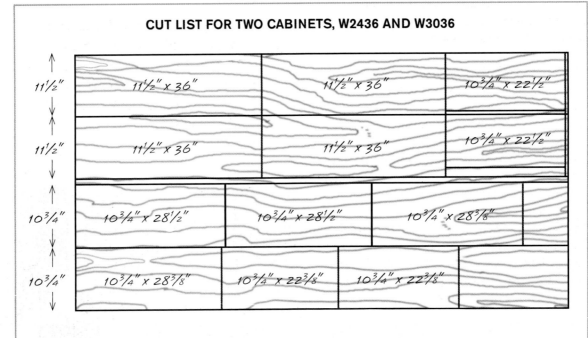

CUT LIST FOR TWO CABINETS, W2436 AND W3036

11½"	11½" x 36"	11½" x 36"	10¾" x 22½"
11½"	11½" x 36"	11½" x 36"	10¾" x 22½"
10¾"	10¾" x 28½"	10¾" x 28½"	10¾" x 28⅜"
10¾"	10¾" x 28⅜"	10¾" x 22⅜"	10¾" x 22⅜"

W2436

- Two 11½" x 36" for the sides ✓
- Two 10¾" x 22½" for the top and bottom ✓
- Two 10¾" x 22⅜" for the shelves ✓

W3036

- Two 11½" x 36" for the sides ✓
- Two 10¾" x 28½" for the top and bottom ✓
- Two 10¾" x 28⅜" for the shelves ✓

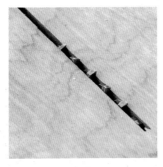

Tearout occurs most often when you are making a crosscut, but it can also happen during rip cuts. Make sure to make test cuts both ways before you start.

If you make label marks on the back edge of your boards, you will not have to sand them off, and they will help you orient the pieces.

then attach the frame, whereas with a frameless cabinet you apply edge-banding to the pieces before assembling the cabinet.

CUTTING THE PIECES

Follow the tips in chapter 4 to cut the parts. Take special care to produce clean cuts and avoid tearout (see p. 53). It's easy to get parts mixed up when you're assembling cabinets, so mark each piece, designating which cabinet and which part it is for. Draw an arrow indicating the face you want to show on the inside of the cabinet.

CUTTING THE DADO FOR THE BACK

Cut a dado groove for the plywood back that is slightly deeper than $3/8$ in. on the inside of each side piece, $1/2$ in. from the back. You can use either a router table or a tablesaw.

tips

A small amount of tearout will not be apparent if the cut edge is covered with a face frame, but imperfections will be on display with a frameless cabinet.

If you get a clean cut with your rip cuts, don't assume that cuts across the grain will also be clean; that's where tearout most often occurs. Test by crosscutting some scrap pieces first.

Choose which side of each piece you want to show. In most cases, that will be the inside of the cabinet. For shelves, the bottom is usually the most visible.

tip

Many $1/4$-in. plywood sheets are actually a bit thinner—often, $7/32$ in. Test the fit with scrap pieces, to see if you need to use a $1/4$-in. or $7/32$-in. bit to cut the dado in the side.

1 To cut the dado for the back with a router table, raise the bit to the correct height. Hold a piece of $1/2$-in. stock between the fence and the bit, rotate the bit so its blade just touches the stock, and tighten the fence in that position.

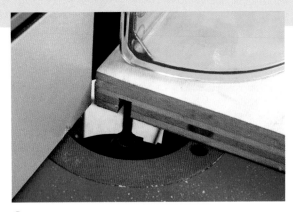

2 Press firmly against the fence as you cut the groove.

3 When you are done, the plywood back should fit snugly, but not so tight that you have to pound it into the groove. If the fit is too snug or too loose, you may need to use a different router bit.

MAKING A DADO WITH A TABLESAW

Producing a dado with a tablesaw calls for two or more passes with the blade. Raise the blade to slightly higher than ⅜ in. above the table. To set the fence for the first pass, position a piece of ½-in. stock between the blade and the fence, and tighten the fence (A). Cut the first pass on a number of pieces (B). To adjust the fence for the second pass, move the fence away from the blade a bit. Put the ½-in. piece in place again against the fence and hold a piece of the ¼-in. stock against it. Move the fence until the ¼-in. stock is flush with the outside edge of the blade (C) and tighten the fence. Make the second cut to finish the dado (D). Test all of your cuts on a scrap piece before cutting on your cabinet stock.

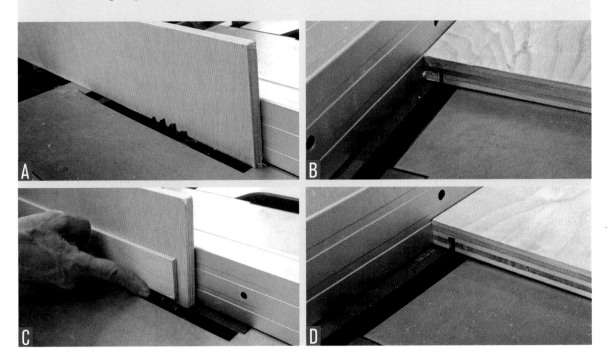

DRILLING ADJUSTABLE SHELVING HOLES

Adjustable shelves will be supported by four shelving pins inserted into holes drilled in the side pieces. The holes must be the exact size of the pins and must be perfectly level with each other.

You can buy guides made for drilling a grid of shelving holes, but many cabinetmakers simply use pegboard, as shown below. Pegboard has a grid of 1/4-in. holes spaced 1 in. apart, which is just right for this purpose. You'll find that 1/4-in. shelf pins are readily available, but if you want to use smaller or larger pins, use a different guide system.

tips

Use 1/4-in.-thick pegboard for a guide. It helps guide you toward drilling straight holes better than 1/8-in. pegboard. Also pay a bit more for tempered pegboard; it's harder than the untempered board and helps keep the bit from wandering as you drill.

Peg holes start and end about 8 in. from the top and the bottom; it's very rare that you would want a shelf above or below those points.

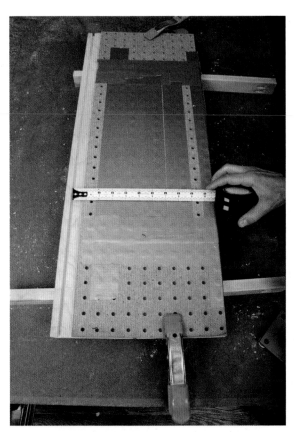

1 Cut a piece of pegboard to use as a guide. Use tape to mark off the holes that will be drilled, so you don't have to think about where to drill. The holes should be between 1 in. and 2 in. from the front and back of the cabinet. Clamp the guide in place.

2 Attach a depth collar to a 1/4-in. drill bit so it will bore a hole deep enough for the pin but will not poke through the plywood.

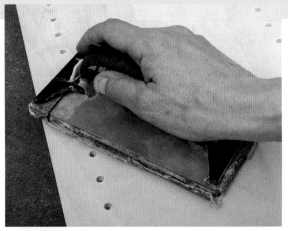

4 Lightly sand the surface to remove all burrs, which can be highly visible once you apply finish. The pins should fit neatly in the holes.

3 Drill the holes, taking care not to bump the guide out of alignment as you work. To drill holes on the other side piece that are level with the first-side holes, flip the guide over and clamp it in the same position (see p. 112).

tip

If you find that pieces wander out of alignment slightly as you drill pilot holes and drive screws, keep them in place with clamps or fasten with pin nails before screwing.

ASSEMBLING THE CASE

For most of the joinery, simply drive screws from the outside of the cabinet. Where a side will be visible and you don't want screw heads to show, use pocket screws, as shown on the facing page. Or use hidden dowels, as shown on pp. 75–77.

Here I assemble a case with unfinished parts, but you may choose to apply finish first. If so, allow it to dry and then assemble as shown in "Assembling a Prefinished Frameless Cabinet" on p. 93. Finish can prevent glue from bonding to wood so make sure to keep it off any areas that you will be gluing.

To keep the cabinet straight and square, continually check with your tape measure and use a square as you work.

1 Where you don't want fasteners to show on the side of a cabinet, drill pocket screws before assembly (see pp. 64–65). Here, pocket holes are drilled in what will be the top of a cabinet.

2 Working on a flat surface, slip the back into the dadoes in the sides and check that the size of the overall cabinet case is correct. If you plan to install a face frame (as shown here but not in the other steps), the frame should overlay the case by ¼ in. on each side when the case is square.

INSTALLING THE BOTTOM ON A FACE-FRAME CABINET

If you will be applying a face frame, the top of the cabinet's bottom piece should be flush with the top of the frame. This will make it easy to slide items in and out of the cabinet. (For a frameless cabinet, simply install the bottom flush with the bottoms of the sides.)

Rip-cut spacer guides to hold the bottom in place as you assemble (A). Set the cabinet's bottom on the spacers and drive pin nails to hold the bottom piece in place (B). Use a spacer as a guide to help you drill pilot holes and drive screws to attach the bottom to the sides (C).

3 Set the top and bottom pieces in place and check for square and that they are the correct size. Apply glue if you wish and drive pin nails or small finish nails to temporarily hold the pieces together. As you work, feel with your hand to be sure the pieces are flush with each other.

4 Drill pilot holes, then drive screws to attach the pieces. On frameless cabinets, take care that the screw heads are flush or below the surface, so they don't interfere with a tight fit to an adjoining cabinet.

tip
If a piece moves out of alignment as you drive a screw, remove the screw, drill another pilot in another location, and fasten again.

5 When joining with pocket screws, be aware that the screws will move the piece with the holes as you fasten. Drive pin nails to position the piece being fastened 1/16 in. to 1/8 in. out of alignment, as shown. Then drive the screws to pull the pieces flush with each other.

6 For the back of the cabinet, cut 1/2-in. plywood cleats to fit snugly between the sides. Apply ample glue to attach the cleats to the case's back. Drill pilot holes and drive screws to attach the cleats to the sides as well as to the top and bottom cabinet pieces.

ASSEMBLING A PREFINISHED FRAMELESS CABINET

If you are building a frameless cabinet, cut the pieces to size and test that they fit together accurately, so everything is square, parallel, and precisely the right size. Install edge-banding (A) and sand so the edges look seamless (B).

For more information about finishing, see chapter 9. Apply a smooth, streak-free finish wherever it will show (C); on the sides that will be covered, it's fine to skip the finishing. Use an artist's brush to apply stain to the inside of holes (D). Assemble with screws and perhaps pocket screws where needed (E).

ATTACHING A FACE FRAME

The most common way to attach a face frame is with pocket screws. Clamp a pocket-screw jig in place and drill pairs of pocket-screw holes (A) the correct size and length for ¾-in. material (see pp. 64–65). Drill pairs of holes spaced 8 in. or so apart. Apply glue if desired, clamp the frame in place, and check that it overlays the cabinet evenly on both sides. (A scrap piece of ¼-in. plywood makes this easy.) Drive 1¼-in. fine-thread screws to attach a hardwood face frame (B).

Where the side of a cabinet will show and you don't want pocket holes, apply ample glue, clamp the frame tightly, and drive pin nails (C). Wait 1 hour or more before removing the clamps, and wait a day before installing the cabinet.

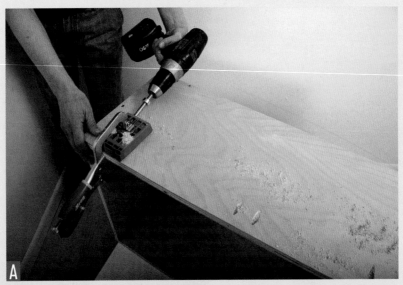

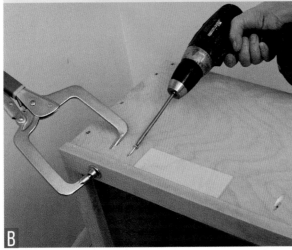

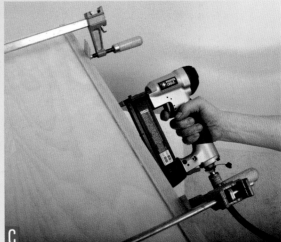

Building a Corner Wall Cabinet

You could simply install basic rectangular wall cabinets so they meet at a corner, but that would lead to wasted space. You could also build a corner wall cabinet similar in shape to the base cabinet design shown on p. 115, but that would make access to the inside space awkward. For the best use of space, build a corner cabinet with a 45° face, like the one shown here, and install a lazy susan inside (p. 178).

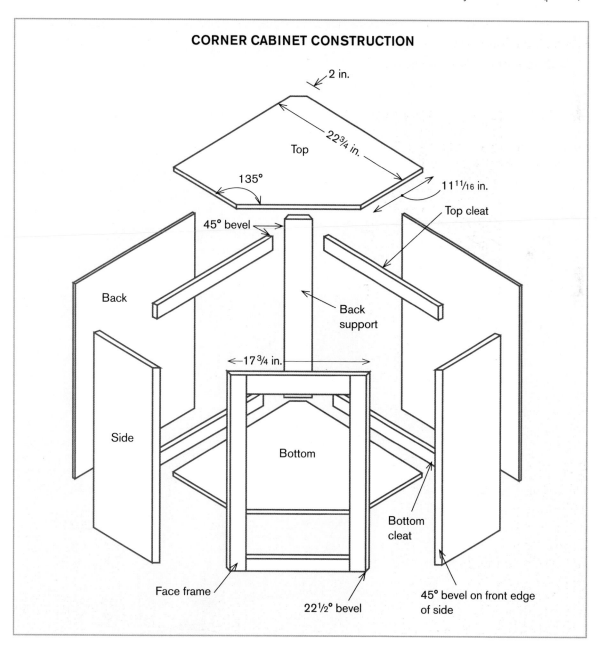

CORNER CABINET CONSTRUCTION

2 in.

Top

22³/₄ in.

135°

11¹¹/₁₆ in.

Top cleat

45° bevel

Back

Back support

17³/₄ in.

Side

Bottom

Bottom cleat

Face frame

22¹/₂° bevel

45° bevel on front edge of side

FACE-FRAME CORNER WALL CABINET, TOP VIEW

¼-in. plywood back

← 24 in. →

← 22¾ in. →

24 in.

Face frame

← 11¹¹⁄₁₆ in. →

Face frames for adjoining cabinets meet with two 22½° bevels.

Wall

FACE-FRAME CORNER WALL CABINET

A corner wall cabinet takes up 24 in. of wall space. Because a face frame overhangs at an angle, figuring this out can be a bit complicated, as you can see in "Face-Frame Corner Wall Cabinet, Top View" at left. But if you carefully cut to the dimensions shown in the main drawing on p. 95, you won't go wrong. (Of course, the length of the sides depends on the desired height of the cabinet.)

In this design, the front edges of the side pieces are bevel-cut to accept the face frame. The sides of the face frame are beveled at 22½°. The face frames for adjoining cabinets will also need to be beveled at 22½°; or you can add spacer pieces, as shown in "If You Want More Space for the Door" on p. 102. The back of the cabinet has a small angled cutout to compensate for irregularities that often occur at wall corners.

A frameless corner wall cabinet is presented in the next section.

tip

Keep in mind that the adjoining cabinets will also need to have their face-frame sides cut at 22^1/$_2$° bevels.

1 Cut a top or bottom piece 24 in. sq. and use a large square to mark for the two angle cuts. The side dimension, from each corner to the beginning of the front angle cut, is 11¹¹⁄₁₆ in. (that is, 11¾ in. minus ¹⁄₁₆ in.).

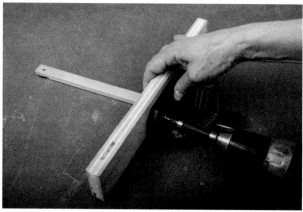

2 If you don't have a large bevel guide for your table-saw, attach a piece of plywood, about 12 in. long, to a standard bevel guide. This will help you keep the sheet correctly aligned as you make the angle cuts.

3 Double-check that the piece is correctly cut. Use the first piece as a template for the second and cut the second piece in the same way.

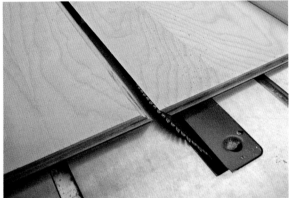

4 Cut plywood for the two side pieces, at least several inches wider than needed, at the desired height of the cabinet. Set your tablesaw to cut at a 45° bevel. Cut a scrap piece and test to be sure it is precisely 45° and make any needed adjustments (left). Then bevel-cut one side of a side piece but keep it 1 in. or 2 in. wider than needed (right).

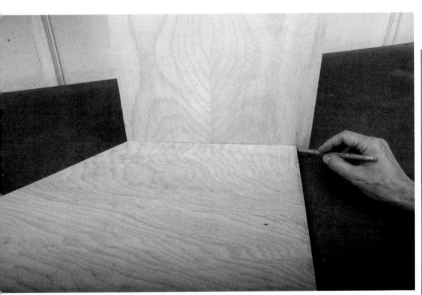

5 Set a side piece in position against the bottom piece so the side piece's beveled side aligns with the angle cut of the bottom. Mark the side piece as shown for cutting to width. Make the cut with a tablesaw.

6 Attach the side pieces to the top and bottom. Use a spacer guide to raise the cabinet's bottom so it will be flush with the top of the face frame bottom.

7 The back support fits between the top and the bottom pieces, so it is about 2 in. shorter than the sides (depending on the amount you raised the bottom piece in Step 6). Cut a piece to length, then bevel-cut one side at 22½°. Hold it in place to mark for the other bevel cut. Attach with screws driven through the top and the bottom pieces.

8 The four nailing cleats span between the sides and the back support. Hold a strip about 4 in. wide in place and mark for cutting. Bevel-cut on a chopsaw or tablesaw and attach with screws.

tip

The screws attaching the cleats to the back should be driven at a slight angle, as shown above. Their heads do not have to be driven flush because this will be blank space.

9 Cut ¼-in. plywood panels to size for the backs. These pieces can overlay the back support slightly. Attach with glue and screws.

10 The sides of the face frame need to be at 22½° bevels. Set your tablesaw to that angle, cut two test pieces, and hold them in place as shown in the top photo; the second piece should be at a right angle to the cabinet. If not, make small angle adjustments as needed. Then bevel-cut the face frame sides.

11 To determine the exact length of the top and bottom frame pieces, hold (or pin-nail) a beveled side piece in place and measure as shown to find the precise position of the side piece; its corner should be exactly 24 in. from the side. Do the same on the other side. Now you can measure between the two side pieces for the length of the top and bottom pieces.

12 Assemble the face frame as shown on p. 72, with the bevel facing down. Drill pocket screws and attach the rails to the stiles with 1¼-in. fine-thread screws.

Building a Frameless Corner Wall Cabinet

When you cut a sheet for the sides at a 45° bevel, the result is an edge that is extra wide and sharp on one side. This is why when building a frameless cabinet, it's a good idea to avoid exposed bevel cuts, and this design does just that.

Because you will be building a pretty simple box that is 24 in. sq., cutting and assembly are straightforward. Start by cutting the top and bottom pieces as in the "Face-Frame Corner Wall Cabinet, Top View" on p. 96. Then cut the side and back pieces, and check that the side pieces will have front edges that are flush with the angle cut of the top and bottom pieces. Cut two stiles that are 2 in. wide to the desired height of the cabinet minus 1½ in.

Test-fit the pieces and check that they will produce a unit that is exactly 24 in. in both directions. Apply edge-banding to all exposed edges: the front edges of the stile and side pieces as well as the front edges of the top and bottom pieces.

Assemble the basic box without the stiles or angled backers, checking for square and correct size as you build. To cut angled backers, rip-cut a piece of 2× lumber at 45°. Fasten the backer to the inside of the side pieces, just a touch back from the front edge, then fasten the stiles to the backers so they are flush with the front of the top and bottom.

tip

If your wall at the corner is wavy or out of level, you may want to cut an angle out of the back corners of the top and bottom pieces and install a short back support piece, as in the design for the face-frame wall corner cabinet on p. 96.

IF YOU WANT MORE SPACE FOR THE DOOR

With full overlay doors, it's possible that the corner unit's door may interfere with the door of the adjoining cabinet. To give the doors a little breathing room, bevel-cut and attach a spacer piece.

FRAMELESS CORNER WALL CABINET, TOP VIEW

24 in.

23¼ in.

11¼ in.

24 in.

2 in.

Stile

Door

45° angled backer

FRAMELESS CORNER WALL CABINET

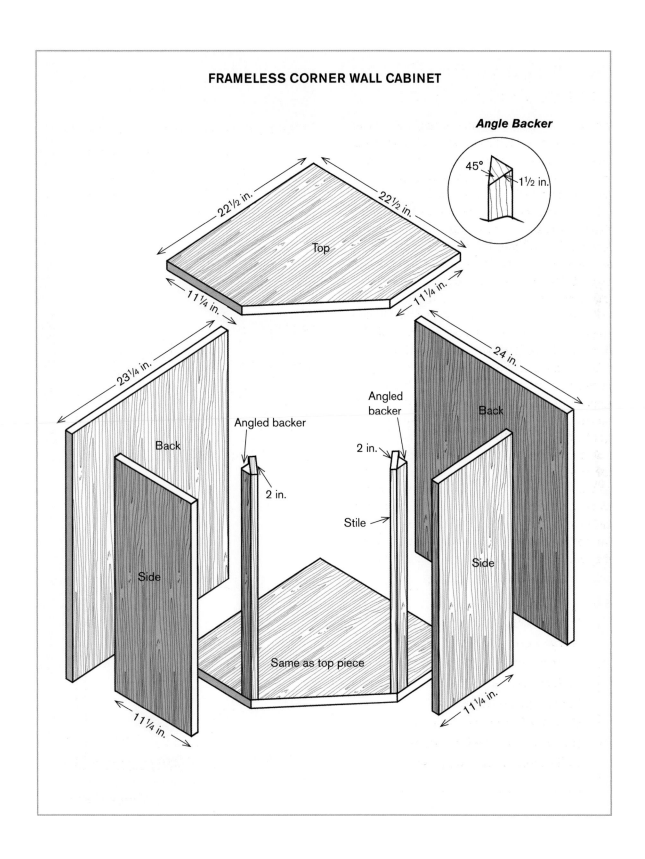

Angle Backer

45°   1½ in.

22½ in.   22½ in.

Top

11¼ in.   11¼ in.

23¼ in.

24 in.

Back

Back

Angled backer

Angled backer

2 in.

Side

2 in.

Stile

Side

Same as top piece

11¼ in.   11¼ in.

1 Attach the side pieces flush with the 45° corner of the base and top piece.

2 Cut the angled backer out of a piece of 2× lumber. It will not be visible in the final cabinet unless you stick your head in the cabinet and crane your neck.

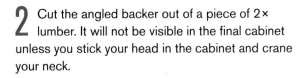

3 Attach the angled backer just slightly behind the side piece, so it will not be visible but so the stile's front edge will be almost fully visible.

4 Attach the stile with pin or finish nails and screws. If you are building with melamine, attach with screws and paint or cover the screw heads.

7

base cabinets and drawer bodies

THOUGH THEY are larger than wall cabinets, base cabinets are no more difficult to build. In fact because they rest on the floor and you don't have to worry about them pulling away from the wall, design is often simpler.

Many of the procedures for building base cabinets are the same as those for wall cabinets. There's no need for complicated or elegant joinery—not even the back dado I recommend for wall cabinets. And almost all the fasteners will be hidden once installed. So although cutting must be precise and pieces must be aligned perfectly, the actual process of fastening can go very quickly.

If you are building with face frames, you'll want to review chapter 5.

Drawer bodies are included in this chapter because drawers are usually found only in base cabinets. Since drawer faces are essentially small doors, they will be covered in the next chapter.

Getting Ready

Follow the tips in chapter 1 for carefully planning the size and placement of all the base cabinets. Be sure the cabinet doors will be able to open next to the range, dishwasher, and walls as well as at any corners. Decide how you will finish the cabinets and perhaps apply the finish before you assemble the cabinets or purchase prefinished plywood.

tips

Plumbing and electrical lines, as well as a hose for the dishwasher, will likely run through some of your base cabinets. In most cases you will cut holes for these after building the cabinets, but check for their locations as you plan.

- - - - - - - - -

A standard base cabinet with one drawer and one door is identified with the letter *B* followed by the cabinet's width. A drawer base (with three or four drawers) is referred to as *DB* and a sink base, which has doors but no drawer, is *SB*. So for instance, DB18 is an 18-in.-wide drawer base and B24 is a 24-in.-wide base cabinet with one drawer.

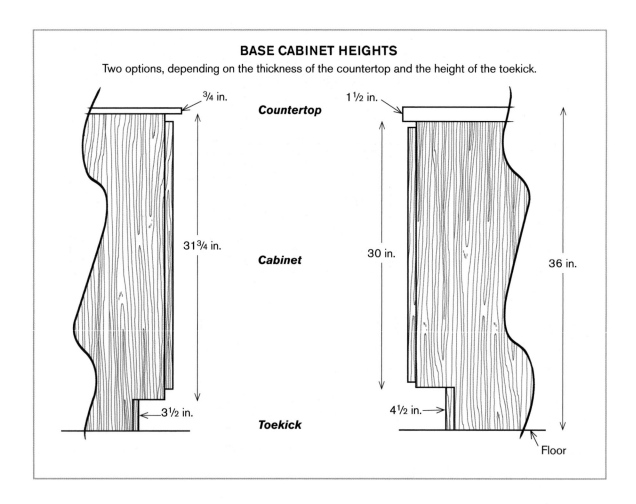

BASE CABINET HEIGHTS
Two options, depending on the thickness of the countertop and the height of the toekick.

¾ in.

Countertop

1 ½ in.

31¾ in.

Cabinet

30 in.

36 in.

3½ in.

Toekick

4½ in.

Floor

BASE CABINET DIMENSIONS

There are a number of variables that will determine the size of your base cabinets.

Height. Base cabinet height depends on the height of the toekick and the thickness of the countertop, as shown in "Base Cabinet Heights" above. Assuming you want the countertop to be 36 in. above the floor, subtract the thickness of the countertop (which may be anywhere from ¾ in. to 1½ in.) and the height of the toekick (usually 3½ in. or 4½ in.) from 36 in. to get your cabinet height.

Depth. Assuming a standard countertop depth of 25 in., total base cabinet depth is usually 24½ in., including the thickness of the door. So a frameless base cabinet is typically 23¾ in. deep and a face-frame base cabinet is typically 23 in. deep.

The frame will add ¾ in. of thickness. If you build with a ¼-in. plywood back (with its edge exposed, so it adds to the depth of the cabinet), subtract ¼ in. from the width of the cabinet sides. If your countertop is wider or narrower than 25 in., adjust the depth of the cabinets accordingly.

tip

Check each plywood or melamine sheet carefully for dents, chips, and other damage. Usually, with careful planning an imperfect area can be hidden—for instance, by placing it at the outside back of a side or at the bottom or top.

CUT LIST AND CHART FOR BASE CABINETS

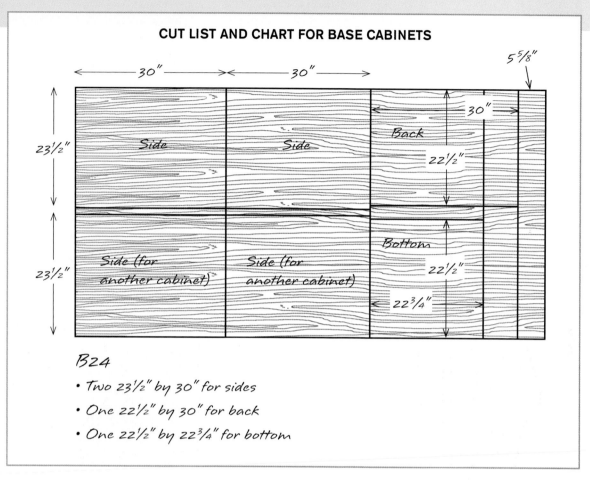

B24
- Two 23½" by 30" for sides
- One 22½" by 30" for back
- One 22½" by 22¾" for bottom

CUT LISTS AND CUT CHARTS

As you would for wall cabinets, make drawings and cut lists for your base cabinets and plan how to cut the pieces out of the sheets most efficiently. Sides for base cabinets are a bit narrower than 24 in., which makes efficient use of 48-in.-wide sheets. The illustration below shows a plan for cutting a single sheet to produce all the pieces for a B24 cabinet, plus two sides for another cabinet.

Base Options for Base Cabinets

Bottom supports for base cabinets are often added after the cabinet cases have been built, but you need to plan for them ahead of time. Many older base cabinet cases are made with notched sides that reach down to the floor, as shown at right.

BASE CABINET WITH NOTCHED SIDES

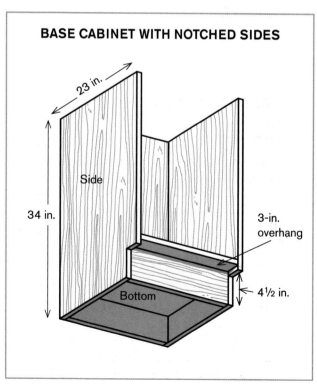

Some cabinetmakers still build that way, but nowadays it's more common to build a simple box to rest on supports. This is a quicker way to build and install the cabinet and a more efficient use of expensive hardwood plywood. Usable space inside the cabinet remains the same.

LEVELING LEGS

You can buy inexpensive adjustable cabinet leveling legs from online sources if your home center does not carry them. To install them, draw a line parallel to the front of the cabinet, at the desired depth of the toekick space plus the ¾-in. thickness of the kick plate. Screw the legs along the line, and in the back as well, as shown in the photo at bottom left. A corner cabinet like the one shown requires eight legs; a standard base cabinet needs only four.

Turn the legs so they are all at the same height, and set the cabinet in place. To adjust cabinet height and bring the cabinet level, screw or unscrew some of the legs. After installing the cabinet, attach the provided clips to a kick plate and snap it in place (see the photo below).

With the kick plate installed, the leveling legs will no longer show underneath the cabinet.

Screw leveling legs in place on the bottom of the cabinet to raise the cabinet high enough to accommodate a toekick.

tip

Leveling legs with snap-on kick plates allow you to easily pull off a plate, giving you easy access to the space below the cabinet for adjusting utility lines or for cleaning. You may even use the space behind a kick plate to store seldom-needed items.

tip

The kick plate that you attach to the leveling legs or to the face of a frame does not need to fit snugly between the floor and the bottom of the cabinet. A gap at the top, of $1/2$ in. or so, will not be noticeable.

CONTINUOUS FRAME

The method outlined here makes it easy to install a series of cabinets that are all level and at the same height. Build a simple frame out of inexpensive wood (see the photo at top right). If you want a $3\frac{1}{2}$-in.-tall toekick, you can build simply using 2×4s. Build a frame with crosspieces every 16 in. or so; there is no need to position the crosspieces to support the sides of cabinets.

Place the frame on the floor and use shims to bring it to level (see the photo at bottom right). Attach the frame to the wall with screws and to the floor with angle-driven screws. Place the cabinets on top of the frame and check for level and alignment. Remove the cabinets one at a time, apply a bead of construction adhesive to the tops of the frame, and set the cabinets in place. Attach the cabinets to the wall and to each other. Apply a finished piece of 1× lumber to complete the kick plate.

This simple toekick frame was built out of 5/4 decking ripped $4\frac{1}{2}$ in. wide. Using inexpensive wood for the frame just makes sense because it will not be seen. A finished piece of 1× lumber underneath the cabinet will complete the look.

Frameless Base Cabinets

Building base cabinets calls for many of the same cutting and fastening methods used for wall cabinets. You can simply drive screws for most of the joints and use pocket screws where you don't want screw heads to show. There is no need to set the back piece in a dado because weight placed in a base cabinet will not pull it away from the wall.

We'll first build a frameless cabinet, then a face-frame cabinet.

BUILDING THE CABINET

In the design shown in "Frameless Base Cabinet 1" below, the cabinet's back as well as its sides and bottom are made of $3/4$-in.-thick sheet stock. The design shown in "Frameless Base Cabinet 2" at right has a $1/4$-in. back, saving on materials if you are using expensive hardwood plywood. In both designs, you will need a stretcher placed at the top and another positioned below it, $1/2$ in. lower

tip

If you are building with melamine, the design shown in "Frameless Base Cabinet 1" below left is better than the method shown "Frameless Base Cabinet 2" below right because $1/4$-in. melamine is prone to cracking, and $3/4$-in. melamine is inexpensive.

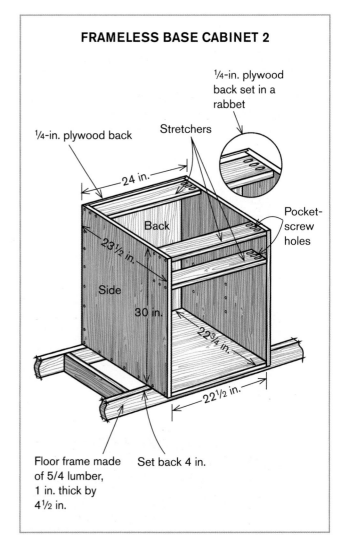

FRAMELESS BASE CABINET 2

$1/4$-in. plywood back set in a rabbet

$1/4$-in. plywood back

Stretchers

Pocket-screw holes

24 in.

Back

$23\frac{1}{2}$ in.

Side

30 in.

$22\frac{3}{4}$ in.

$22\frac{1}{2}$ in.

Floor frame made of 5/4 lumber, 1 in. thick by $4\frac{1}{2}$ in.

Set back 4 in.

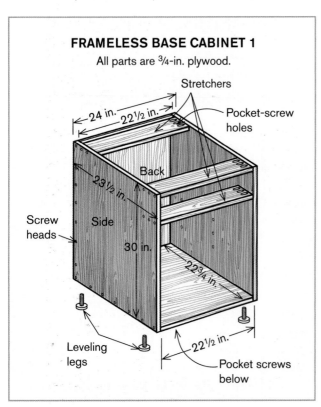

FRAMELESS BASE CABINET 1

All parts are $3/4$-in. plywood.

Stretchers

Pocket-screw holes

24 in.

$22\frac{1}{2}$ in.

Back

$23\frac{1}{2}$ in.

Screw heads

Side

30 in.

$22\frac{3}{4}$ in.

Leveling legs

$22\frac{1}{2}$ in.

Pocket screws below

than the height of the drawer you plan to install. You also will add a single stretcher in the top back. You can set the cabinet on leveling legs or on a continuous frame.

The following steps are for the first design but most of them apply to the second as well. To start, cut the sides, back, and bottom pieces. Cut the two front stretchers, which can be anywhere from 3 in. to 7 in. wide. The rear stretcher can be made of scrap material because it won't show. Apply edge-banding to the front edges of all the pieces except the rear stretcher.

PARTIAL-SHELF OPTION

Though it's not as popular as it used to be, many people find that a partial-depth shelf in a base cabinet has accessibility advantages, making it easy to see and reach things in the back of the bottom shelf. Holes drilled for a partial-depth shelf will not interfere with other storage options such as a slide-out shelf, so cabinetmakers often provide the holes to leave the option open.

1 Use a simple peg-board jig and a drill bit with a depth collar (see p. 89) to drill a series of holes for a half shelf in the side pieces. Typically, the front holes are positioned at about the center of the side pieces to accommodate a shelf that is about two-thirds the depth of the cabinet. Use the pegboard guide on one side piece, then flip it over to drill holes in the other side to mirror the holes in the first piece.

2 Lay the bottom on a flat surface and attach the sides and the back. Where a side will not show, simply drive screws. Check for square and feel with your finger to be sure pieces are aligned as you fasten. Drill pilot holes before driving screws or use self-tapping screws.

3 Where a side will be exposed, fasten with pocket screws from the back (see pp. 64–65). Adjust the drill depth carefully and drive 1¼-in. coarse-thread screws. Test on scrap pieces to be sure the screws will fasten securely without poking through.

4 Install the top front stretcher. Cut a scrap piece that is ½ in. longer than the desired height of the drawer and clamp it below the top stretcher as a spacer when you attach the bottom stretcher.

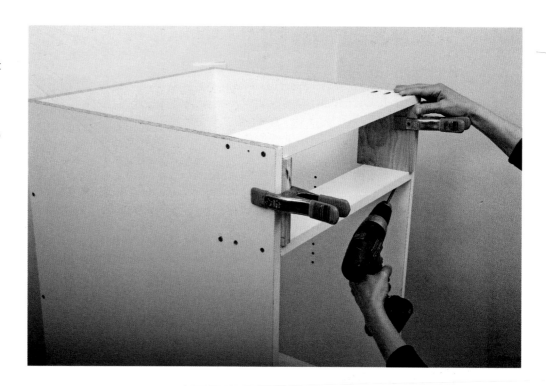

5 Attach a rear stretcher, which can be made of scrap plywood, to make the cabinet rigid and to keep it square while it is being installed.

6 Add leveling legs or build a continuous frame on the floor to raise the cabinet to the correct height.

Face-Frame Base Cabinet

Building with a face frame is similar to building the frameless base shown in the last section (in this example I'll show a narrower cabinet for variety). See chapter 5 for building face frames. Besides not having to apply edge-banding, there are two main differences: The sides will be ¾ in. narrower (see "Face-Frame Base Cabinet Dimensions" at right), and there is no need for a lower front stretcher for the drawer; the face frame takes care of that.

Attach the face frame as you would for a wall cabinet (see p. 101). Use pocket screws where the side of the cabinet will not show and glue and pin nails where the side will show.

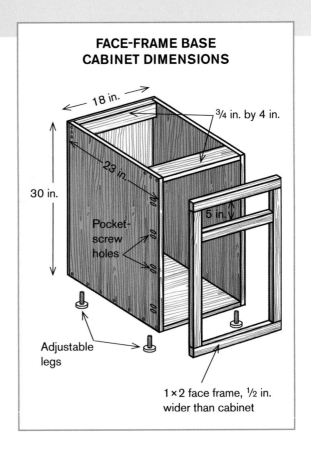

FACE-FRAME BASE CABINET DIMENSIONS

18 in.

¾ in. by 4 in.

23 in.

30 in.

5 in.

Pocket-screw holes

Adjustable legs

1 × 2 face frame, ½ in. wider than cabinet

BASE FACE FRAMES AND THE BOTTOM SHELF

The base cabinet's bottom shelf should have its top flush with the top of the bottom rail of the face frame, so you can easily slide items in and out. However, the face frame is usually thicker than the plywood used for the bottom shelf. There are two ways to deal with this.

The face frame is often installed so it underhangs the cabinet, as shown at right. Assuming a 1½-in.-wide face frame, it will underhang by ¾ in. (If you use wider stock for the face frame, this underhang will of course be larger.) This method works well if your base frame or leveling legs are, say, 4½ in. or taller.

But if your base is a 2×4, then building with an underhanging face frame would create a toekick only 2¾ in. tall, which is uncomfortable. You may want to raise the bottom shelf ¾ in., as shown at far right.

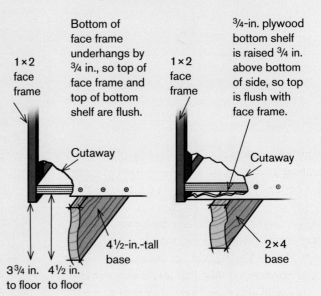

INSTALLING BASE CABINET FACE-FRAMES AT THE BOTTOM

For clarity, the face frame parts are colored.

1 × 2 face frame

Bottom of face frame underhangs by ¾ in., so top of face frame and top of bottom shelf are flush.

Cutaway

3¾ in. to floor

4½ in. to floor

4½-in.-tall base

1 × 2 face frame

¾-in. plywood bottom shelf is raised ¾ in. above bottom of side, so top is flush with face frame.

Cutaway

2 × 4 base

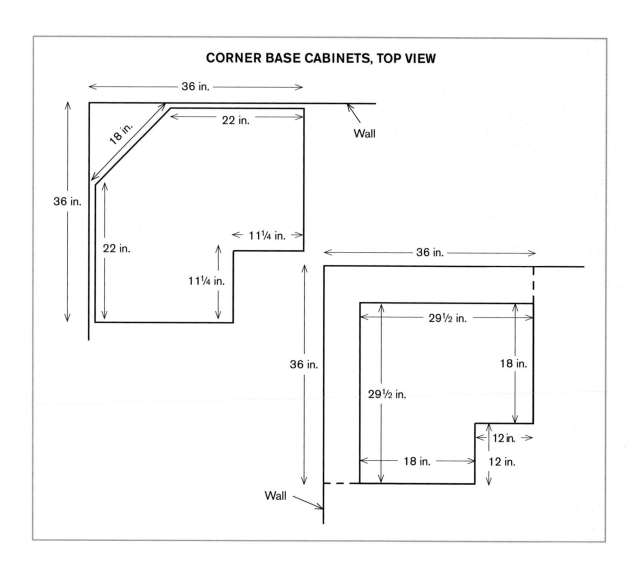

CORNER BASE CABINETS, TOP VIEW

36 in.

22 in.

18 in.

Wall

36 in.

22 in.

11¼ in.

11¼ in.

36 in.

36 in.

29½ in.

18 in.

29½ in.

12 in.

18 in.

12 in.

Wall

Corner Base Cabinet

As with a corner wall cabinet (see pp. 95–104), for planning purposes a base cabinet needs to take up a certain amount of wall space—usually, 36 in. in each direction. However, corner base cabinets rarely extend all the way back to the wall.

Corner base cabinets are sometimes made with angled fronts like the wall corner cabinet shown on p. 95. However, building that way means the countertop would also need to be angled—and would therefore need to be wider than the standard 25 in.

at the corner. So it is common to build base corner cabinets with a 90° front cutout.

Such a cabinet can be equipped with a lazy susan; the door front may be double-hinged to gain easy access to the opening or the lazy susan itself may have an angled door that swings inside the cabinet when you rotate it.

This means that unlike with a corner wall cabinet with an angled front, you don't need to do any fancy calculating when planning a base cabinet. The illustrations above show two different base cabinet designs in relation to the walls. As long as the front cutout opening is the same dimension in both directions, a base cabinet can slide into position and takes up 36 in. of wall space but is only 18 in. deep.

Buy your lazy susan ahead of time or read its installation manual carefully to be sure it will fit into the cabinet you build. Make sure the cutout opening is the correct size and that the inside dimensions are large enough.

CORNER CABINET WITH SHELF

If you don't mind bending over and maybe getting on your knees to reach things or if you have storage items that you need to get at only a couple times a year, you could go with a shelf instead of a lazy susan. This design, with a single shelf off to one side, makes it relatively easy to reach into the back corner, and allows for storing tall objects on one side.

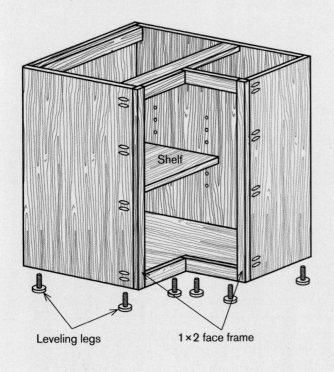

Leveling legs   1 × 2 face frame

Large Frameless Base Corner Cabinet

The design shown here has plenty of space for a large lazy susan. It's angled in the back, to eliminate dead space where things can fall off the lazy susan and get lost.

Fastening a lazy susan directly to the underside of a countertop is an iffy proposition at best. So one of the stretchers at the top is extra-wide, to provide a fastening surface for a future lazy susan. Consult manufacturer's instructions to be sure you will be able to securely install the unit you've selected.

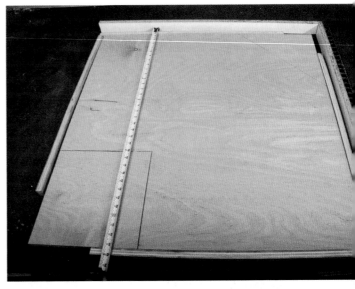

1 Cut a base piece square and large enough for your purposes. Here, the base is 33 in. sq. Mark for a cutout in front that will give you plenty of access and will be the correct size for your lazy susan or shelf, if any. Also mark for an angled cut in back; again, make sure your shelf or lazy susan will fit. Remember that after the sides are installed, the overall cabinet size will be 1½ in. wider in each direction than the base. For the project shown here, the sheet to be used for the base is placed next to white pieces of melamine, representing the wall, to confirm it fits within a 36-in. wall space.

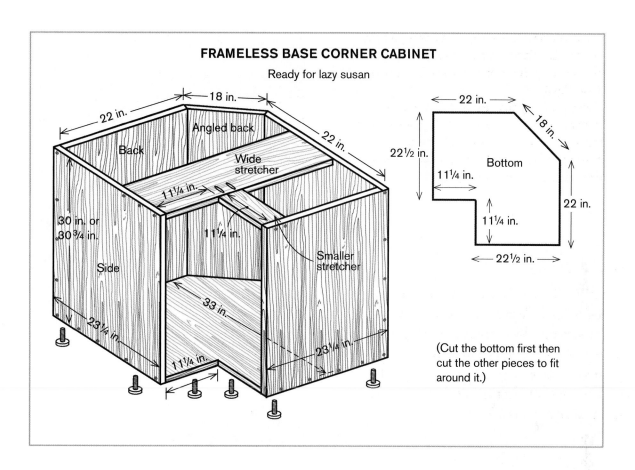

FRAMELESS BASE CORNER CABINET

Ready for lazy susan

Back

Angled back

Wide stretcher

Smaller stretcher

Side

18 in.

22 in.

22 in.

11¼ in.

11¼ in.

30 in. or 30¾ in.

23¼ in.

33 in.

23¼ in.

11¼ in.

22 in.

18 in.

22½ in.

11¼ in.

22 in.

11¼ in.

22½ in.

Bottom

(Cut the bottom first then cut the other pieces to fit around it.)

2 The large angle cut may be difficult to make on a tablesaw, so clamp a straight piece to act as a guide and cut with a circular saw. Cut the front notch in the same way or with a tablesaw.

3 Cut the side pieces and two of the back pieces (but not the angled back yet) to fit. Apply edge-banding to the front cutout of the base and the forward edges of the sides.

4 Assemble each side-and-back combination. Support one of the pieces and check for square as you drive the screws.

5 Set the bottom on a flat surface and attach each side-and-back combination with screws. Check that the edge-banded surfaces are flush with each other as you fasten.

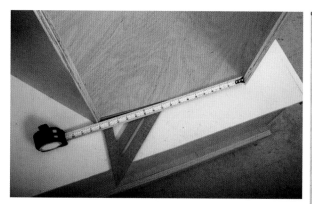

6 Measure for the angled back and cut it at a 45° bevel on each side.

7 Fasten the angled back with screws driven at slight angles, as shown. The screw heads will not drive flush, but that doesn't matter because they will be in dead space at the back of the cabinet.

tip

After marking the wide stretcher in Step 8, you may find it easier to remove the wide stretcher and drill the pocket holes on a worktable, then replace the wide stretcher and drive the pocket screws.

8 Cut a wide stretcher, the same length as the base, and fasten with screws on each side. Cut a smaller stretcher the same length as the front cutout. Make a mark on the wide stretcher to show where to attach the small stretcher, to ensure the pieces will mirror the cutout in the base piece. Fasten the small stretcher to the cabinet side with screws and to the wide stretcher with pocket screws.

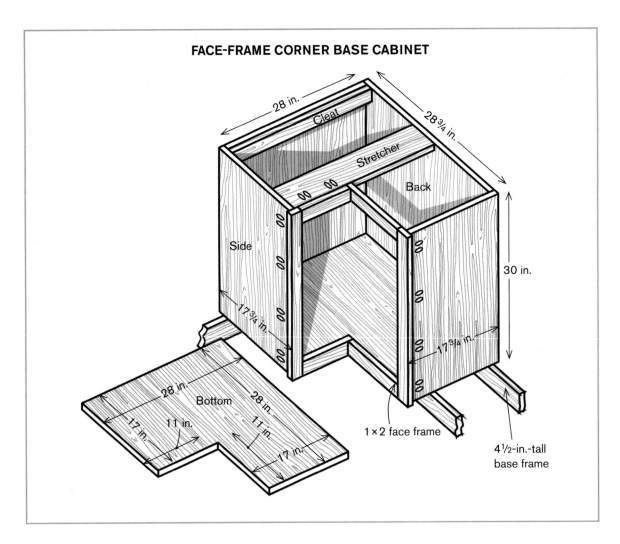

FACE-FRAME CORNER BASE CABINET

28 in.

Cleat

28 3/4 in.

Stretcher

Back

Side

30 in.

17 3/4 in.

17 3/4 in.

28 in.

Bottom

28 in.

17 in.

11 in.

11 in.

17 in.

1 × 2 face frame

4 1/2-in.-tall
base frame

tip

For this cabinet, the exact dimensions of the opening are not critical (as long as they are the same in each direction). You could either build the face frame first or build the cabinet and then make the face frame to fit.

Building a Face-Frame Corner Base Cabinet

A face-frame corner base cabinet is built very much like a frameless one. The example shown here is only 17 in. deep, which is smaller than the one shown in previous pages. It can be made out of a single sheet of plywood or melamine.

Cut the bottom to the size needed for your lazy susan or shelf, keeping in mind that the face frame will make the opening a bit smaller. Working on a flat surface, fasten the sides, then the back pieces. To the back, attach a cleat at the top to one side only. Cut and install a stretcher wide enough to provide a fastening surface for your lazy susan, if you will have one.

If you haven't already done so, build a face frame following "Face-Frame Corner Base Cabinet" on the facing page. Cut the horizontal rails ¾ in. shorter on one side than the other, so the finished opening will be the same in both directions. Fasten the rails to the stiles with pocket screws and fasten the rails to each other at the inside corner by drilling pilot holes and driving screws from the back. Use pocket screws to attach the frame to the stretcher, the sides, and the bottom. One rail can run unsupported at the top.

Drawer Bodies

A drawer body is a simple box that fits into a base cabinet opening that is created by the face frame or by stretchers in the case of a frameless cabinet.

A drawer face, made to coordinate visually with the cabinet doors, will be installed later (see chapter 8).

To determine the drawer's width, check the instructions for the drawer glides you plan to install. Inexpensive nylon-runner glides take up ½ in. on each side, so the drawer body should be 1 in. narrower than the opening. Ball-bearing glides generally take up half the space, allowing for wider drawers that are ½ in. narrower than the opening. If you use side-mounted glides (the most common type), the drawer body should be at least ½ in. shorter than the opening.

The most common drawer depth (that is, its horizontal length) is 22 in., though it can be a bit longer or shorter. Again, check your glide hardware.

Drawers are used and abused many thousands of times and so need to be reliably rigid and sturdily built. Most designs feature a combination of snug-fitting dado joinery and carefully driven screws to achieve durability.

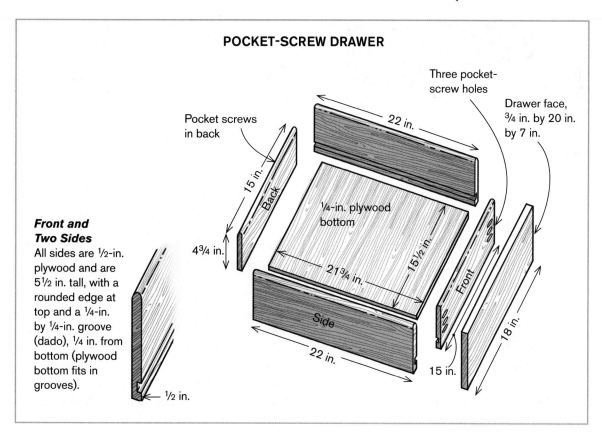

POCKET-SCREW DRAWER

Three pocket-screw holes

Pocket screws in back

Drawer face, ¾ in. by 20 in. by 7 in.

22 in.

15 in.

Back

¼-in. plywood bottom

4¾ in.

Front and Two Sides
All sides are ½-in. plywood and are 5½ in. tall, with a rounded edge at top and a ¼-in. by ¼-in. groove (dado), ¼ in. from bottom (plywood bottom fits in grooves).

21¾ in.

15½ in.

Front

Side

22 in.

18 in.

15 in.

½ in.

Building a Pocket-Screw Drawer Body

The method shown in this section makes quick work of drawer building. As "Pocket-Screw Drawer" on p. 121 shows, the $1/4$-in. plywood bottom fits into a dado on three sides, pocket screws attach the sides to each other, and the back of the drawer is rip-cut and fastened from below with nails or screws driven through the bottom.

1 Rip-cut the stock to the desired width ($1/2$ in. shorter than the opening's height). Sand the edges smooth. For a more finished look, use a router with a roundover bit to finish the top edge.

2 Use a router table to rout a dado for the plywood bottom or cut the dado with two or more passes using a tablesaw (see p. 88). The groove is $1/4$ in. above the bottom of the stock and just wide enough for the plywood bottom to fit snugly.

3 Cut the pieces. The two sides are the length of the drawer body and the front and back are 1 in. shorter than the width. Stacking and cutting, as shown, is an easy way to cut two boards to the same length.

4 Rip-cut the back piece along the top of the dado, so it can sit on top of the plywood bottom and be the same height as the sides.

5 Keep the parts organized and mark them to be sure they will be installed in the correct order.

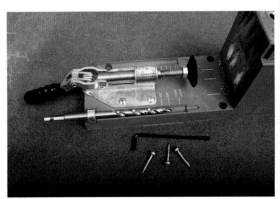

6 Set the pocket-screw bit to the correct length for attaching ½-in. stock. You will use 1-in. coarse screws. Drill three fairly evenly spaced pocket holes on either side of the front and back pieces.

7 Using a right-angle clamp, as shown, drive pocket screws to attach the front to the sides. Check for square as you go, but the clamp should keep things pretty straight and installing the bottom (Step 9) will effectively square the drawer.

tip

When working with ½-in. stock, pocket joinery must be precise or the screws can produce unattractive protrusions. Before you actually build a drawer, practice on scrap pieces until you are sure the drill bit is set to precisely the correct depth and you can make clean-looking, firm joints.

8 Cut the plywood bottom to fit, taking special care to keep it perfectly square on all four sides. Cut it about ¹⁄₁₆ in. shorter and narrower than the opening; one way to do this is to cut through the middle of the cut line, as shown.

9 Slide the bottom into the grooves from the back toward the front. The bottom should fit snugly and only gentle tapping should be needed.

10 Apply glue, taking care not to glue the bottom, and fasten the back with pocket screws.

12 Once you are certain the drawer is square, turn the drawer over and fasten the bottom to the back with small screws. Drill pilot holes to prevent splitting.

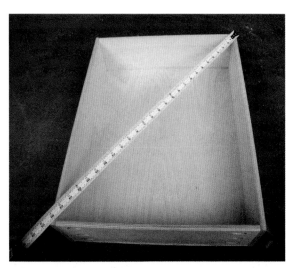

11 Make a final check for square by measuring the diagonals; they should be exactly the same length.

tip

If the drawer is not square, you may be able to tap one corner (using a block to prevent marring the wood) to align it. If that doesn't work, remove and recut the bottom.

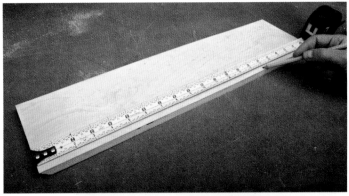

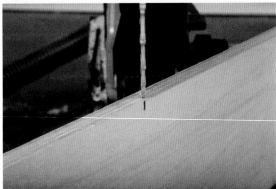

1 Use a tablesaw or a power miter saw to cut 45° bevels on both sides of all four pieces. Each piece is cut to the desired length or width of the drawer.

tips

If a local hardwood supplier sells precut drawer sides, as shown on p. 42, buying them will save you the trouble of rip-cutting, making dadoes, routing, and sanding. They come only in certain sizes, so be sure the cabinet opening will accommodate them.

It is critical for this design that all the miter cuts be precise. Test each cut for square. You may want to clamp the piece in place when cutting with a miter saw to prevent wandering.

Mitered Drawer

Using miters is simplicity itself and creates a drawer body with a crisp, clean appearance. If you execute the joints carefully, with pilot holes just the right size and driven nice and straight, the result will be durable.

Start by rip-cutting ½-in. stock to the desired height of the drawer body. Sand the edges smooth and, if desired, rout the top edge with a roundover bit; a rounded top looks particularly attractive on a miter-jointed box.

2 To mark the drawer bottom for cutting, slip the bottom into the dadoes of a side piece and either the front or back and draw a cut line that is about ¹⁄₁₆ in. short of the end of the dado, as shown. Cut the bottom on a tablesaw, making sure it is perfectly square.

3 After you've cut the bottom, test-assemble the five pieces to be sure they fit. If a joint cannot be pushed together tightly, you may need to recut the bottom. Measure the diagonals to be sure the box is square.

4 At each corner, use a corner clamp to keep the sides aligned as you drill three pilot holes through the front or back and into a side piece.

tip

If a board jumps out of alignment while you drill a pilot hole, do not use that hole; drill another one nearby.

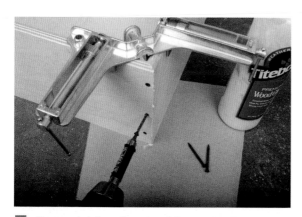

5 For each joint, disassemble, apply glue, and drive 1⅝-in. square-drive trim-head screws to produce a tight joint.

6 Wipe away most of the squeezed-out glue immediately. Allow the glue to dry, then sand the edges smooth.

Routered Drawer

Routing is a classic way to build drawers that has proven itself over the decades. This type of drawer can be easy to build if you have the equipment to quickly make dadoes and rabbets. If you start with precut drawer sides (see p. 42), you need make only ½-in.-wide dadoes and rabbets.

Rip-cut and dado the ½-in. drawer stock. Cut the sides to the desired length of the drawer, and cut the front and back to the desired width, minus ½ in.

On each side piece, cut a ½-in.-wide rabbet in the front inside edge and a ½-in.-wide dado in the back, ½ in. from the back of the piece. Cut the ¼-in. plywood bottom to fit in the grooves, with ¹⁄₁₆ in. to spare in each direction, for expansion.

Test the assembly; all the pieces should fit snugly but not too tightly. Disassemble, apply glue to the joints, reassemble, and drive three finish nails into each joint.

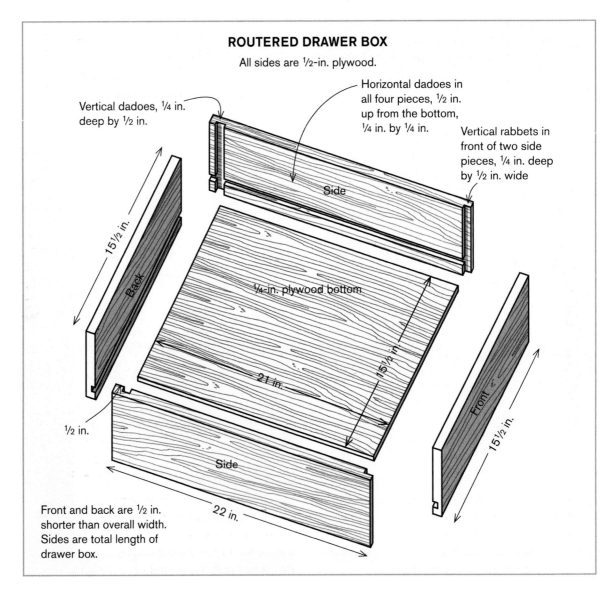

ROUTERED DRAWER BOX

All sides are ½-in. plywood.

Vertical dadoes, ¼ in. deep by ½ in.

Horizontal dadoes in all four pieces, ½ in. up from the bottom, ¼ in. by ¼ in.

Vertical rabbets in front of two side pieces, ¼ in. deep by ½ in. wide

Side

15½ in.

Back

¼-in. plywood bottom

15½ in.

21 in.

Front

15½ in.

½ in.

Side

22 in.

Front and back are ½ in. shorter than overall width. Sides are total length of drawer box.

Drawer with Locking Joint

This section details a time-honored joinery method that was once primarily made by hand or with a tablesaw, but a special router bit makes it easier. With the use of a drawer-lock router bit you can make tight-fitting joints at all four corners of the drawer box. The effect will be subtle but distinctive.

Before working on a drawer, test your skills on scrap pieces of ½-in. stock until you are sure you can produce tight joints.

Start by ripping the stock to the desired height of the drawer. Rout a groove for the drawer bottom.

tip

Be sure to buy a drawer-lock router bit that will work with ½-in. stock; some types work only with thicker boards.

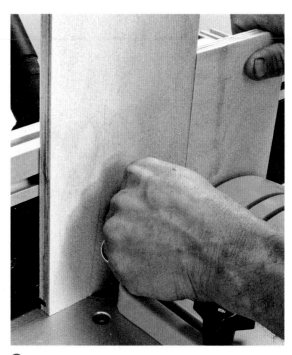

1 The drawer-lock bit comes with a spacer block for quickly adjusting the router bit height and the fence position. Use it to set the router bit at ⅜ in. above the table (top). Then use the same tool to position the fence (above).

2 Cut grooves in the ends of the side pieces first. Use a featherboard or press steadily to achieve a groove that is consistent in depth. You can do this cut in one pass. Keep the router bit at the same height for the remaining heights.

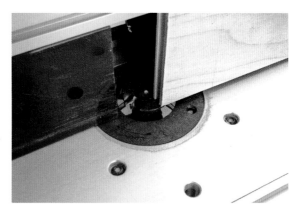

4 The last pass for the groove on the face and back pieces should cut a groove exactly ½ in. deep. Hold a piece of stock as shown to measure for the correct depth.

3 Cut both ends of both the face and back pieces. This is a deeper cut, so you may need to move the fence slightly toward you, rout the groove, then turn off the router and follow Step 4 to position the fence for the final cut.

tip

If you don't have a spacer block, you can use a straightedge along with a scrap of ³/₈-in.-thick plywood or a tape measure to set the bit at ³/₈ in. above the table and the fence at ³/₈ in. behind the forward-most part of the bit.

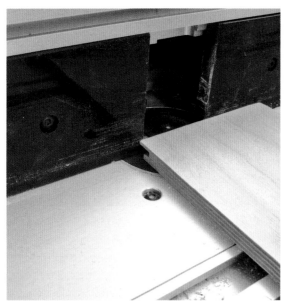

5 Cut both sides of the face and back pieces to the final groove depth of ½ in., as shown in Step 4. The finished pieces should fit together neatly and tightly.

doors and drawer faces

CERTAINLY THE most visible parts of kitchen cabinets—and even the most visible elements of the kitchen as a whole—are the cabinet doors and drawer faces. The cabinet cases and drawer bodies are generally plain and boxy, to maximize their storage capacity. The doors and drawer faces express the overall style of your work.

The most common doors are made with frames and panels. This style of construction is more complicated. But this chapter will show you how to build a variety of styles for the frames. If you choose raised panels, you will probably need a router and router table. Plywood panels are much simpler. Building frames and panels calls for careful joinery. If you are doing this for the first time, you will find yourself learning a good number of new techniques. Allocate plenty of time, so you can enjoy the process rather than feel harried.

In addition to standard frame-and-panel doors, I'll show a few approaches that are definitely easier. For instance, slab doors are simplicity itself, cottage-style doors can be made quickly, and there is even a type of frame-and-panel door that can be made with a tablesaw only—no router required.

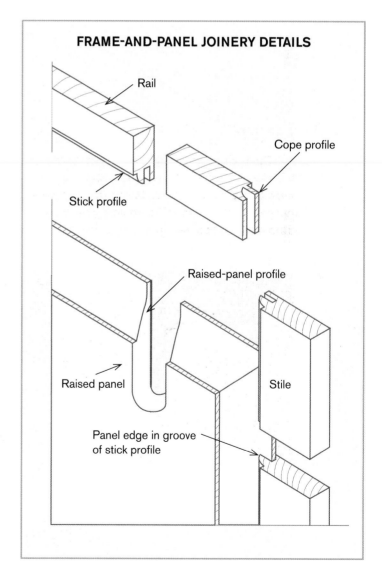

FRAME-AND-PANEL JOINERY DETAILS

Rail

Cope profile

Stick profile

Raised-panel profile

Raised panel

Stile

Panel edge in groove of stick profile

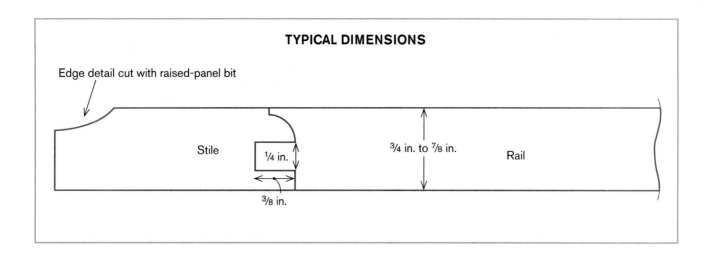

TYPICAL DIMENSIONS

Edge detail cut with raised-panel bit

Stile

¼ in.

⅜ in.

¾ in. to ⅞ in.

Rail

Planning Frame-and-Panel Doors

A frame-and-panel door is composed of a center panel and a surrounding frame made with two vertical stiles and two horizontal rails. Usually, the stiles are as long as the door is tall; the rails fit between the stiles. The panel may be made of plywood, which is usually ¼ in. thick (or slightly thinner), or it can be a raised panel made of thicker stock.

UNDERSTANDING THE PARTS

Rails and stiles as well as raised panels are generally made of material that is ¾ in. to ⅞ in. thick. If you buy dimensional 1× lumber from a home center or lumberyard, it should be consistently ¾ in. thick. If you buy from a hardwood supplier, the thickness may vary. It's important that all the parts (not including a plywood panel, if you are using that) be the same thickness. If necessary, use a thickness planer, as shown on p. 29, to mill the parts as needed for consistent thickness.

On a raised panel, the edges are routed to produce a decorative profile on the perimeter. This profile ends at a thickness of ¼ in., or slightly thinner, to fit into a routed groove on the inside edge of the frame pieces.

DOOR FACES THAT HARMONIZE

If a drawer face is narrower (shorter) than 8 in., it usually looks best to make it out of 1× material that matches the door panels. Rout the edges with the same bit used to rout the outside of the door frames or a bit specifically made for drawer edges. (Do this even if your door panels are plywood.) You could also choose to build wider drawer faces with frames and panels that match the doors.

tip
A flat Shaker-style door can be made with a tablesaw only; no routing is required. See p. 138.

Two different routed profiles allow the stiles, rails, and panels to fit together. The *stick profile*, cut along the inside edge of both the stiles and rails, includes a groove into which the panel can fit. The ends of the rails also have a *cope profile*, which nests neatly into the stick profile of the stiles.

CHOOSING THE PROFILES

The look of frame-and-panel doors is determined by the router profiles you choose as well as the width of the frame parts.

There are four profile choices to make:

- For the frame, choose a set of matching router bits that produce stick and cope profiles that fit together. See "Common Stick and Cope Profiles for Frame-and-Panel Doors" below for the most popular styles.

- Decide on the look of the door's perimeter. You may decide to leave it squared off and unrouted, which is the usual choice for Shaker doors. Or you may just slightly round over the perimeter.

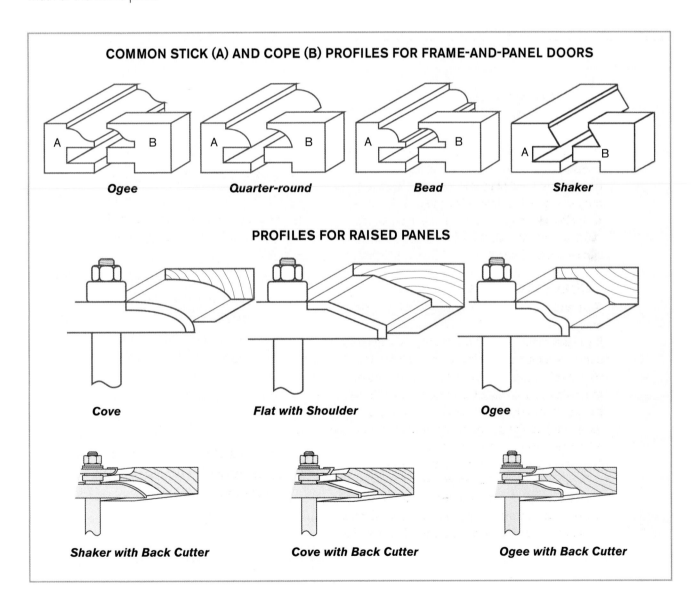

COMMON STICK (A) AND COPE (B) PROFILES FOR FRAME-AND-PANEL DOORS

Ogee   *Quarter-round*   *Bead*   *Shaker*

PROFILES FOR RAISED PANELS

Cove   *Flat with Shoulder*   *Ogee*

Shaker with Back Cutter   *Cove with Back Cutter*   *Ogee with Back Cutter*

ROUTER SPEEDS AND THE RIGHT ROUTER

The wider a router, the slower it should spin. If a bit spins faster than the recommended speed, it will likely burn the wood or cause chipping or tearout. Some bits come with literature telling you the recommended speed, but many do not, so here are some general guidelines.

RECOMMENDED SPEEDS

Bit Diameter	Maximum Speed
1 in. (25mm)	24,000 rpm
1¼ in. to 2 in. (30mm to 50mm)	18,000 rpm
2¼ in. to 2½ in. (55mm to 65mm)	16,000 rpm
3 in. to 3½ in. (75mm to 90mm)	12,000 rpm

Because you will be using bits of various diameters, you need a variable-speed router for this type of work. And to cut at lower speeds, the router should be powerful—at least 2¼ hp. (If your router is not variable speed, you may be able to use a vertical panel-raising bit, as shown on p. 136.)

Or select a router bit that harmonizes with the appearance of the stick profile.

- Also choose the profile for the raised panel (unless you will use plywood panels). Be sure the panel will fit into the groove of the stick profile on the frame. For the best appearance, select a bit with a back cutter; this allows the panel's face to be on the same plane as the frame, rather than recessed.

- Finally, select a profile for the perimeter of the drawer faces. This may exactly match the profile of the door perimeters or it may be less pronounced, but it should be in a design that harmonizes with the doors.

FRAME WIDTH

The frame's rails and stiles can range from 1½ in. to 2½ in. wide. This is a matter of personal taste. However, you may want to simplify door calculations by choosing a frame width that is, say, the width of the cope profile plus an even 1 in. or 2 in. If you plan to build a door with a curved top stile, that piece will of course need to be wider.

tip

It's difficult to describe the decorative effects of various router profiles, but here's a stab at it. Ogee and bead profiles are fairly Victorian and have an old-fashioned appeal. Quarter-round and cove profiles are more modern and are sometimes considered Craftsman or Deco in appearance. Shaker style, which is unrouted, has simple, clean-looking lines that may look modern or cottagey, depending on the finish of the wood.

BUYING ROUTER BIT SETS

Buy router bit sets at a woodworking store or from online sources. Be sure to check customer reviews before you buy. Many inexpensive bits will dull quickly and may not even cut well the first time. But don't assume you have to buy the most expensive: Some mid-priced bits can give years of clean cuts.

- If you're using plywood panels, you need a minimum of two matched bits, one for the stick cut and one for the cope cut. You may also want a bit or two to rout the perimeter of the doors and the drawer fronts.

- A three-bit set typically routs the stick and cope cuts as well as a raised panel. In some cases you can use the stick bit to rout the door and drawer face perimeters as well. Or you may buy one or two additional bits for those elements.

- A six-bit set can be a good value. In addition to the stick, cope, and raised panel bits, it may include both a drawer front and a door edge bit as well as a pattern cutting bit for making arch-top doors.

CHOOSING LUMBER

For general tips on selecting boards and plywood sheets, see chapter 3. It's important that your lumber be straight and dry. Boards should have a moisture content of 15% or lower; otherwise, they can warp and shrink after installation. Sight along the length of a board to ensure that it is flat along its length. Also use a straightedge along its width to check for cupping. If a board is seriously cupped, either do not buy it or plan to thickness plane it.

A pin-type moisture tester gives a fairly accurate indication of a board's moisture content.

CALCULATING PART SIZES

Sizing door parts can get complicated, so take the time to double-check your figures before you start cutting the pieces.

Overall door size. First, determine the overall size of the door. Nowadays most doors are full overlay, meaning they are larger than the cabinet's openings and partially cover the cabinet's frame (or, in the case of a frameless cabinet, they partially cover the cabinet's front edges). A ½-in. overlay on all four sides is common; it means the door will be 1 in. lon-

ger and wider than the inside of the cabinet opening. If you want your doors to overlay the cabinet frame by more or less, be sure to take that into account.

Stiles. This is simple. The stiles are cut exactly to the desired height of the door.

Rails. These are the most complicated to figure. Rails fit between the stiles, so their length depends on the width of the stiles as well as the length of the cope cut's tenon (its longest part) on each end of the rails. Make a cope cut on a scrap piece and measure its length, as shown below.

This cope cut's tenon (its longest part) is ⁷⁄₁₆ in. long. That means the pieces for the rails will be cut ⁷⁄₈ in. (2 × ⁷⁄₁₆ in.) longer than the distance between the stiles.

VERTICAL PANEL-RAISING BITS

If your router is not variable speed, you may still be able to use it for a raised-panel door. Vertical panel-raising bits do not require a variable-speed router. First, make sure that the stick and cope bits are of the recommended diameter for your router's speed (see "Router Speeds and the Right Router" on p. 134). Then find a vertical panel-raising bit that works with your router's speed.

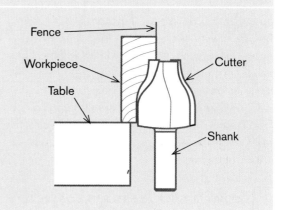

tip

You may be able to simplify your calculations when you choose the width of your stiles. For instance, if the stick cut's tenon will be $7/16$ in. long, rip-cut stiles that are $2\,7/16$ in. wide. That would make your "magic number" simply 4: Cut the rails to the width of the door, minus 4 in. Easy peasy! Alternatively, cut a scrap piece to twice the tenon length and use it when measuring rails.

To measure the depth of a groove, insert a piece of plywood or other thin wood into the groove, scribe a line, pull out the plywood, and measure.

Once you know the length of the cope cut, here's the formula:

> **Width of the door − Width of both stiles + Length of both cope cut tenons = Rail length**

For example, if a door is 18 in. wide, the stiles are $2\,1/4$ in. wide, and the cope cut tenons are $7/16$ in. long, the rail length will be $14\,3/8$ in. long:

> **18 in. (overall width) − $4\,1/2$ in. (2 × width of the stiles) + $7/8$ in. (2 × cope cut tenon length) = $14\,3/8$ in. (rail length)**

Panels. Cabinet doors are typically built so the panel has room to expand in width during times of high humidity. That means the panel should be $1/8$ in. narrower and shorter than the distance from groove to groove in each direction. And it means the panel width is the length of the rails minus $1/8$ in. However, if a panel is wider than 18 in., most cabinetmakers allow for a greater gap—from $3/16$ in. to $1/4$ in.

Wood barely expands lengthwise, along its grain. That means the height of the panel is the distance from rail groove to rail groove. However, $1/16$ in. is often subtracted from the height to ensure an easy fit. Follow this formula:

> **Door height − (2 × Rail width) + (2 × Groove depth) − $1/16$ in. = Panel height**

For example, if a door is 27 in. tall, the rails are $2\,1/4$ in. wide, and the groove is $1/4$ in. deep, the panel height will be $22\,15/16$ in.:

> **27 in. (overall height) − $4\,1/2$ in. (2 × rail width) + $1/2$ in. (2 × groove depth) − $1/16$ in. (for ease of fit) = $22\,15/16$ in. (panel height)**

Sorting and Listing

Even a modest-size kitchen will have quite a few doors and drawer fronts, so start by getting organized. Use the calculations on this page to create a cut list:

- Figure the overall sizes and add up all of your doors and drawer faces.

- Determine the width of all your rails and stiles. Figure the lengths (remember, stiles are the exact height of the doors and the rails are shorter).

- Determine the number and sizes of the panels. If they will be plywood, make cut charts so as to get the most panels possible out of each sheet. Unless you will paint, all panels should be cut with the grain running vertically.

- If your panels will be raised, making a cut list is more complicated. You'll need to find out the widths of the boards you will use (these can vary, especially if you get boards of various widths from a hardwood supplier). Plan for boards with grain patterns that look good together side by side. Also try to reduce waste as much as possible.

- Plan your drawer faces. These will be of various sizes, and some may be simple routed slabs while others may be frame and panel.

Shaker Doors with a Tablesaw

Shaker doors with plywood panels, which might be the most popular style of cabinet door these days, can be made without a router or router table. An accurate-cutting tablesaw is all you need. You can also make a raised panel using only a tablesaw (see pp. 151–153).

(see pp. 151–153).

1 Cut the two stiles and two rails to length, following the calculation guidelines on p. 137. (You could also make this cut using a tablesaw.)

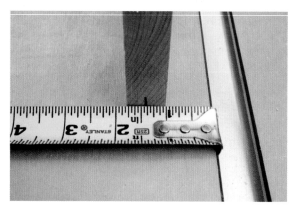

2 To cut the groove for the panel with a standard tablesaw blade, mark the middle of a rail's or stile's thickness. (In this example, the board is $13/16$ in. thick; the center mark is between $3/8$ in. and $7/16$ in.) Raise the tablesaw's blade to a height of $3/4$ in. You can use a piece of $3/4$-in. plywood to make this measurement. (Don't use a piece of rail or stile material unless it is exactly $3/4$ in. thick.)

following the calculation guidelines on p. 137.

tips

In most kitchens, the great majority of doors are of two sizes—one for base cabinets and one for wall cabinets. If you find the task of planning all the panel pieces and matching grain patterns confusing, you may choose to cut most of the pieces for each size door, then shuffle the pieces around until you get the best looking arrangement.

The cope cut (or tenon) measurement is the length of the tenon (which is also the depth of the groove). In our example, that is $3/4$ in. on each side, so you cut the rails to the overall width of the door minus twice the width of the stiles plus twice the length of the tenon, or $1^{1}/_{2}$ in.

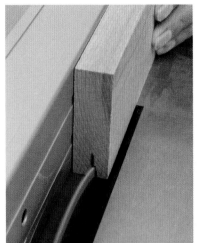

3 *Do this first with a scrap board the same thickness as your rails and stiles. Don't cut the groove on the real framing pieces until you are certain of the fence position.* Set the tablesaw's fence so the blade cuts on one side of the center mark (left). Press the board tightly against the fence and firmly down on the table as you cut a groove all the way through. Turn the board end to end and cut again the same way (middle). If there is a sliver remaining in the middle, place a thin spacer against the fence and cut the sliver out (right).

4 Slip a piece of the plywood you will use into the groove you just cut. It should be snug, but not so tight that you need to hammer hard to force it in. If the groove is too narrow, move the saw's fence ever so slightly away from the blade and cut the same groove again. If the groove is too wide, move the fence slightly in toward the blade and cut a new board. Keep experimenting until you get the fence in the precise position to cut the perfect-size groove.

tip

> The width of the groove depends on the thickness of the plywood. Standard $^1/_4$-in. plywood is usually thinner than an actual quarter inch. In this example, I use Baltic birch plywood, which is a full $^1/_4$ in. thick.

You may be able to cut the groove using a dado blade set, with two blades only. With the set I'm using, two blades with the required spacers make a groove just the right thickness for $^1/_4$-in. Baltic birch.

5 To cut the tenons on the ends of the rails, install a set of dado blades on your tablesaw. Remove the standard blade and follow the manufacturer's instructions for installing an outer blade, spacers, inner chippers with spacers, and another outer blade. Make the total thickness of the dado setup no thicker than the tenon (in this case, ¾ in.).

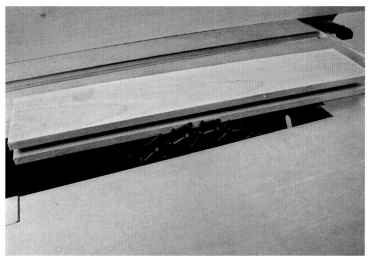

6 Clamp a board to the side of the fence, so the dado blades cannot hit the metal fence. Raise the blades so they will cut just to the bottom of the groove (above). Measure and set the fence so as to cut a tenon the desired length (right).

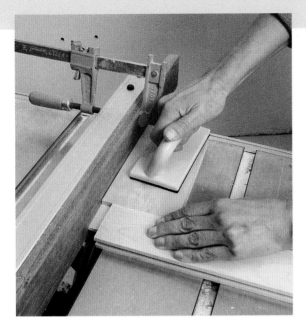

tip

If your dado set produces a cut that is a bit jagged, you may need to recut as you push the board in and out from the fence in order to smooth it out. Keep the board flat on the table and aligned with the square wood block as you do this.

7 *Again, follow these instructions on scrap boards the same thickness as the door frame and cut tenons on the actual rails only after the fence is precisely aligned at the correct position. To cut the tenons, hold a rail perpendicular to the fence and use a square wood block with a push tool as shown to cut each side of the tenon.*

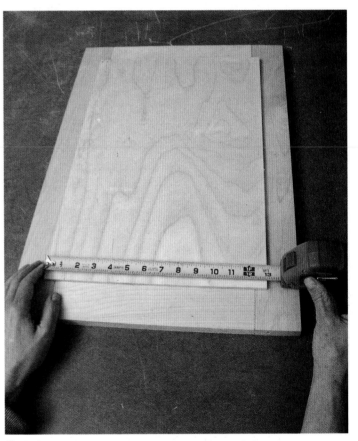

8 Assemble the frame pieces and check that the frame is the correct size and is square.

9 Cut the plywood panel so it is ¼ in. narrower and shorter than the distance from groove to groove. If the groove is ¾ in. deep, the plywood should be 1¼ in. wider and longer than the inside of the frame. (In the photo, the cut plywood is ⅝ in. wider than the inside dimension.)

10 Dry-fit the panel and frame pieces and check for correct size, tight joints, and square. Disassemble and apply glue to the rail tenons only. Do not get glue on the panel because it needs to be able to expand and contract slightly with changes in humidity. Fit the pieces back together and clamp the two ends with medium pressure only; clamping too tightly will squeeze out too much glue.

11 Drive a couple of ⅝-in. pin nails into each joint from each side. Many cabinetmakers skip this step, but it adds firmness.

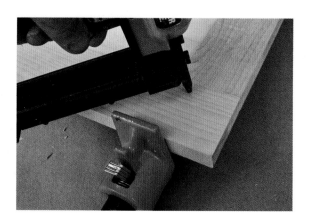

Routing Rails and Stiles

Rails and stiles can be routed to accept either a plywood or a raised panel. As long as you use a matching set of router bits and cut at the same level, the cope and stick joints will fit together neatly. It's a very good idea to practice on scrap pieces until you get the knack.

tip

Most cabinetmakers cut the copes first, then the stick profiles, but some do it the other way round.

1 Raise the bit to the right height and position the fence so it is flush with the bit's bearing. On this bit, the bearing is in the middle of the two cutters.

2 To minimize tearout at the end of the cut, use a sacrificial backer board. The backer board should be cut square, to help align the rail. Push the rail through in one smooth stroke. Cut both cope cuts for both rails.

BIT GAUGES

Some router bit manufacturers offer bit gauges, which make it easy to get your bits to the correct height. The gauge seen here, by Sommerfeld, can be adjusted to cut boards of various thicknesses and it fits with eight different profiles.

MATCHING HEIGHTS

To line up the stick-cutting router with the cope cut, it often helps to align its cutter with the tongue of the cope cut.

3 Set up the stick bit and the fence so it aligns with the cope cut. Then cut scrap pieces and make adjustments until you get a stick profile that matches the cope. Rout the inside edges of the rails and stiles.

ROOM FOR EXPANSION

To keep the panel firmly in place while at the same time permitting it to expand and contract, place special foam strips like these in the grooves of the rails and stiles. Another option is to use Space Balls® (spaceballs .com), which are pretty much the same thing, only spherical.

4 Dry-fit the four pieces to see that they fit well. If you are installing a plywood panel, cut it to size (1/8 in. short in both directions) and assemble the door. If you are installing a raised panel, see "Jointing and Gluing Up Raised Panels" on p. 146.

5 To assemble a door, apply glue to the cope cuts only. Be sure not to get glue on the panel because it needs to be able to expand and contract slightly with changes in humidity. Check for square and clamp the frame in two places. For a firm joint, clamp with light to medium pressure, so you don't squeeze out all the glue.

tip

> To permit the panel to move inside the frame, ideally the panel and the frame will each be separately coated with finish and allowed to dry before assembly. In practice, that can be difficult to achieve. But you may be able to apply a finish, or part of a finish, to one or more components before assembly (see p. 162).

OTHER PROFILE POSSIBILITIES

Here are two popular frame-and-panel door configurations. The door made with ogee bits (top) has a rounded outer edge on the frame. The cove door (bottom) in this example has a panel made from MDF.

Jointing and Gluing Up Raised Panels

You can skip this section if you plan to use plywood panels or if you will be making a raised panel from MDF. You can sometimes make narrow door panels out of a single wide piece of lumber. Often, however, you will need to glue two or more pieces side by side. Choose boards that look good next to each other.

PANELS THAT ARE FLAT

If you start with lumber that is flat across its width (that is, not cupped) and if all the pieces are precisely the same thickness, then you can often simply glue them together to produce a panel that is quite flat; then, only a modest amount of sanding will be needed to make it perfectly smooth.

However, if boards are cupped or of varying thickness, you'll need to do some thickness planing. A modest-size thickness planer will plane individual boards but will plane full panels only if they are 12 in. or narrower. So unless you have a big expensive thickness planer that can handle wider pieces, you'll need to plane individual pieces, glue them up carefully so they are level with each other, then sand or scrape the resulting panel.

> **tip**
>
> Using a jointer works well as long as the board is nearly straight to begin with. But if the board is significantly bowed, you will have to run the board through the jointer a number of times. Many cabinetmakers will sometimes joint warped boards with a tablesaw even if they have a jointer.

> **tip**
>
> A hardwood supplier will often smooth one edge of its boards for free. However, this usually means smoothing only and not jointing. So unless the board was very straight to begin with, you may need to joint anyway.

JOINTING

The edges of the panel's boards must be perfectly straight, so they will line up side by side tightly all along their lengths, with no visible gaps. If you buy dimensional lumber (with smooth edges) that is really straight, you may be able to just cut the pieces to length and glue them together. Often, however, even dimensional lumber is not straight enough to glue up, and you will need to joint the edges. And lumber bought at a hardwood store will certainly need to be jointed.

Jointing is the process of smoothing a board's edge and cutting it precisely straight. This can be done with a jointer or with a router table that has jointing capabilities (see p. 28). A jointer removes only a small amount of material—perhaps 1/16 in.—at a time.

You can also do this with a tablesaw that has a smooth-cutting blade and a simple jointing jig, as described in the next section.

JOINTING WITH A TABLESAW

When a board is bowed, you can't use either edge as a guide for straightness, which means you can't simply cut with the board running against your rip fence. You need a jig that holds the board straight as you cut. That type of jig (it can also be called a sled) is easy to make.

1 Rip a piece of plywood that has a factory edge (which is precisely straight) about 3 in. to 4 in. wide. Rip another piece about 8 in. wide. (If you will be jointing wide boards, rip it wider.) Glue and screw the narrow piece on top of the wide piece, with the top piece's factory edge along the edge of the bottom piece. To make sure the factory edge will slide along the tablesaw's rip fence, make it flush with the lower piece or have it run past the lower piece by 1/16 in. or so.

Add a few plywood blocks on top of the jig, and attach toggle clamps (also called hold-down clamps) to them. These will hold the board to be jointed in place. Be sure to get the kind of toggle clamps with a handle that you move upward to tighten; if the clamps have a handle that moves down to tighten, the handles will bump into the rip fence.

2 Clamp the board to be jointed so it overhangs the jig. Position the tablesaw's rip fence so that when the jig is pressed against it, the sawblade will cut all along the length of the board you are jointing. Measure at the board's narrowest width; at that point, the sawblade should just barely cut the board.

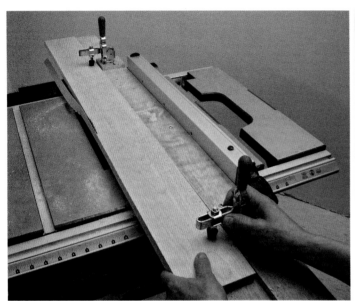

3 Rip-cut the board with the jig pressed against the fence. Aim for a long, smooth cut because stopping and starting can create unevenness. Once one side is jointed, remove the board from the jig and joint the other side by rip-cutting with the tablesaw's fence.

ANOTHER WAY TO JOINT ON A TABLESAW

If you have only a few boards to joint, or if you need to joint a very wide board, the method described here is a good option. Start with a piece of plywood or hardboard with one factory edge. Position the plywood so its factory edge slightly overhangs the board to be jointed, and fasten it with short 23-gauge pin nails that are about 1/2 in. longer than the thickness of the plywood. Place the plywood against the tablesaw's fence and position the fence to cut as little as possible while still cutting all along the length of the board. Make the rip cut, remove the plywood, and pull out the pin nails with a pair of pliers. The nail holes will be virtually invisible.

GLUING

Working from the dimensions you calculated for panel size (p. 137), cut the pieces to the correct size or slightly larger (see the first tip at right). You will clamp the panel about every 12 in., so you will probably need three or four clamps per door. Have your clamps within easy reach, so you can quickly use them once the glue is applied.

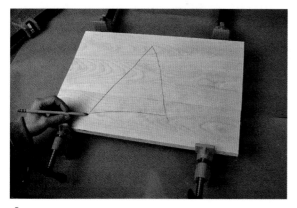

1 Place your panel boards side by side in the desired order and press them together to be sure they will fit with no gaps. Draw a carpenter's triangle on the boards to help reestablish the order as you reassemble.

2 Spread glue fairly evenly along one of the edges for each joint. You can use a glue brush or your finger.

tips

Many experienced cabinetmakers initially cut raised-panel pieces to the correct size and glue them together; then the panel is ready for edge routing. If you are a beginner, are unsure of your skills, or just want to be careful, make your panels about $1/2$ in. longer and wider than they need to be. After the glue has dried, you can cut them to the exact size you want.

You may be tempted to use biscuits, dowels, or other fasteners to reinforce the joints between panel boards. But most cabinetmakers do not do that. Simply gluing up with no fasteners, if done correctly, creates joints that are at least as strong as the wood itself.

Standard woodworking glue, such as Titebond®, is plenty strong for gluing up. If the door will be in a bathroom or other damp place, a waterproof glue (such as Titebond II) is a good choice. Glues with longer setup time (such as Titebond III) are easier to work with but may mean that you have to wait longer before removing clamps.

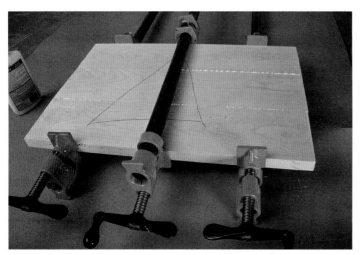

3 Place the boards on the pipes or bars of two clamps. Close the clamps until they just start to pull the boards together. Adjust the board positions so their ends and their faces are flush. Place another clamp in the middle, facing the other direction. This will help keep the panel straight. Tighten the clamps with light to medium pressure—tight enough to make good-looking joints, but not so tight you cup the boards or squeeze out most of the glue, which will make for a weak joint.

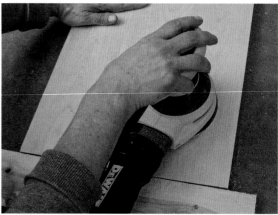

4 Allow the recommended amount of time for the glue to fully harden and then remove the clamps. Remove most of the glue with a wood scraper, taking care not to gouge the wood. If you have a jointer that is wide enough, run the panel through it. If not, sand the surface with a random-orbit sander. Start with 60 grit, then move on to 80 grit, 100 grit, 120 grit, and so on until you achieve the desired smoothness. Continually feel for irregularities with your hand.

5 Cut the panel to the desired final size. Now the panel is ready to be edge routed for a frame-and-panel door.

If the surface is in need of serious flattening, some woodworkers use a smoothing plane (not a block plane or a jack plane) to smooth the surface of a glue-up. Start with strokes that angle across the grain, then plane with the grain for the final smoothing. You may choose to use a sander as well. Another option is to use a belt sander: Work carefully and don't press down or linger in any spot for more than a second because the sander can dig in quickly. Start with 60-grit or 80-grit paper and move up to 100 grit. Then switch to a random-orbit sander.

Shaping a Raised Panel on a Tablesaw

A raised panel must be shaped so its edges will fit into the inside-edge groove of the door's frame. This is often done on a router table, using a bit that's matched to fit the stick profile. However, you can also do this on a tablesaw. The resulting panel has a somewhat geometric rather than a curvy look, which is at home with Shaker and Craftsman styles.

Glue up the panel (pp. 149–150) or use MDF if you will paint the door. Cut the panel to the desired size (p. 137).

AUXILIARY FENCE

To make a wide beveled cut in a panel, first build an auxiliary fence, so you can hold the panel firmly perpendicular to the table. Make the narrow horizontal strip the same height as the fence. Cut all the pieces carefully and assemble on a flat surface so the fence will be perfectly upright. Make the front face from a melamine board or other smooth sheet material. (This fence is seen in Step 3 on p. 152.)

Melamine face   Chip board   Plywood   2-in. screws   30 in.   ¼-in. screws   Plywood   2½ in.   9 in.   30 in.   9 in.   2½ in.   2-in. screws

All parts are ¾ in. thick.

tip

If you will be cutting the grooves in the rails and stiles with a tablesaw (pp. 138–140), it may be easier to cut the panel first and then cut the rail and stile grooves to match.

1 Clamp the saw's fence 2 in. away from the blade and position the blade just ⅛ in. above the table.

2 Run the panel, face side down, along the fence in all four directions. This will produce a crosshatch pattern (as shown in Step 4).

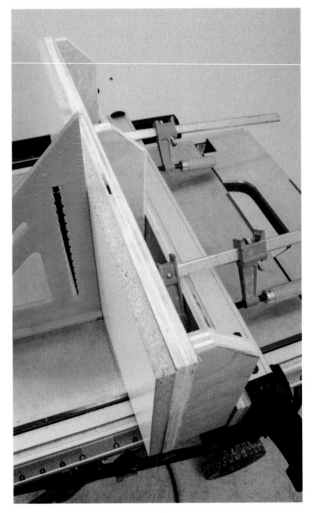

3 Attach an auxiliary fence to the tablesaw's fence and check for square. See "Auxiliary Fence" on p. 151.

4 Adjust the blade angle to 10° and raise the blade to the height of the cut-outs you made in Step 2. Position the fence to cut the panel at the correct thickness on the perimeter so it can slip into the grooves in your rails and stiles.

5 Use a featherboard to keep the panel snug against the fence as you cut. Make one cut and test that the panel will fit into the rails and stiles. Rotate the panel and cut the other three sides.

6 Sand the cut edges with a random-orbit sander, then a hand sander, to remove any burrs. Because you are sanding against the grain, use fine sandpaper.

Routing a Raised-Panel Edge Profile

As long as you use a router bit that matches the one used for the stick profile (pp. 133–135), routing the panel profile is straightforward. Be sure that the bit is at the correct height and the fence is in the correct position; then the profile will automatically fit.

tip

The panel router bit removes a lot of material, so you may have to rout in two or three passes. You could eliminate a pass or two by first cutting away some of the material using a tablesaw. Test on scrap lumber first to be sure you won't cut away too much.

2 If your router is straining, you may need to make three passes. For the final pass, adjust the fence so it is flush with the bit's bearing.

1 If you are using a horizontal router bit with a back cutter, as shown, raise the bit to the desired height of the cut. (For other types of bits, see "Vertical Panel-Raising Bits" on p. 136.) Unless you made a tablesaw cut to remove some material, you will probably need to rout in two or three passes. Start with the fence moved forward a little, so it only partially cuts the profile, as shown. Adjust the router's speed to the manufacturer's recommendation or consult "Recommended Speeds" on p. 134. Cut all four sides. If the router strains to cut, move the fence a touch more forward so it has less to cut.

tip

Routing can cause tearout at the end of a cut across the grain. To minimize tearout, rout a panel in the following order: (1) cut across an end grain side, (2) rotate counterclockwise and cut with the grain, (3) rotate and cut the other end grain side, and (4) cut the last side with the grain.

3 Sand the profile so it is silky smooth. Depending on the profile, you may use a foam sanding block or a firmer block. If you're having trouble smoothing, it can help to wrap a piece of sandpaper around a dowel or a piece of trim, or even to mill a block of wood to match the profile and use that as a sanding block.

4 Dry-fit the door to make sure it fits. Insert foam strips or Space Balls into the grooves (see p. 144). Apply glue to the rail ends only, taking care to keep glue away from the panel, and clamp the two joints.

(see p. 144)

tips

With practice you can learn to place just enough glue in the cope joints, so they will be fully adhered without excessive squeezed-out glue, which is a bit of a pain to sand away.

- - - - - - - -

The outside edge of a door may be left square or you can route a profile that harmonizes with the door's other profiles.

MAKING AN MDF PANEL

MDF is often used for panels that will be painted, but not for frames, because it is a bit too easy to dent. Cutting and routing an MDF panel is easier than working with wood. Tearout isn't much of a problem; the little burrs along the cut edges can quickly be sanded away.

Slab Doors

Slab doors, sometimes called plain or flat-panel doors, need little in the way of instruction because they are simple to make. Yet many expensive and stylish kitchens feature them. Slab doors are generally modern in appearance, especially if they are made with melamine sheets. However, they can lend a surprisingly rich texture to a kitchen when made of plywood with striking grain patterns. See pp. 38–39 for design tips when choosing plywood panels.

PLYWOOD OR MELAMINE SHEET DOORS

It is sometimes feared that a simple sheet of plywood may warp over time. However, cabinetmakers report that good-quality plywood sheets are remarkably stable. Choose sheets that have been stored flat so they are not even slightly warped.

GLUED-UP DOORS

Slab doors can also be made with 1× pieces glued together. A solid door like this can then be edge-routed to any pattern you choose.

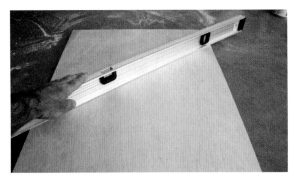

Choose plywood that is perfectly flat; it should have been stored flat (rather than upright) at the lumberyard. It should have a moisture content of less than 15%.

If you plan to stain the doors, pay close attention to the grain patterns and colors. You may choose to have side-by-side doors repeat patterns or mirror patterns. Or you may prefer a random assortment of patterns.

EDGING WITH WOOD

Applying solid wood, rather than veneer edging, to the edges of your panels adds a bit of interest and makes for a door that better resists splintering and chipping. Cut the door ½ in. narrower and shorter than the finished dimensions. Rip ¼-in. strips for the edging and attach them with wood glue and 18-gauge or 23-gauge finish nails. Sand the edges and corners to make them slightly less sharp or use a router to slightly round them over.

Doors and drawer faces will be looked at up close, so take special care when applying edging. Pros often can achieve razor-sharp lines with a knife or chisel, but most of us will get more reliable results using tools made for the purpose. See pp. 57–58 for instructions on edge banding.

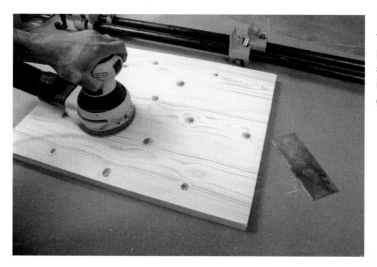

Pattern match, joint, and glue up the doors as you would for a raised panel (pp. 146–150). Make the door slightly larger than needed, then cut it to the finished dimensions after the glue has set.

You can now rout the edges of the door to any pattern you choose.

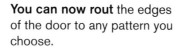

Cottage-Style Door

A cottage-style door typically features knotty wood and tongue-and-groove joints. A simple door can be made quickly with tongue-and-groove paneling.

Paneling wood is not made for cabinetry, so choose the very best boards you can and don't expect perfection. Select boards that are pretty straight, both along their edges and along their faces. Be sure to check the moisture content (see p. 43) and use boards with 15% or less.

Even if you use the best boards available, don't be surprised if a certain amount of warping and cracking occurs. Consider it part of the rustic charm.

1 Cut the pieces to length and assemble them with tongues in grooves. Cut the door to width. Be sure to cut off the tongues and grooves on the outside edges. You may need to have two narrow pieces on each side, or on only one side, in order to get the right width.

Assemble the pieces. Check the door for square and reinforce the back with cleats. The cleats should leave room at the sides to allow the door to close and should not be placed where they will get in the way of hinges. Attach with two screws in each joint. Gluing is not recommended; the boards will expand and contract slightly with changes in humidity.

2 Rout the edges with a door router bit or a roundover bit. Test on scrap pieces first to get the most pleasing depth of cut. Rout across the grain, then rotate the door a quarter turn and rout with the grain, and so on for all four sides. (Ending by routing with the grain reduces tearout.)

3 You'll probably need to do some sanding at the edges. Apply sealer or paint.

Glass Doors

Kitchens often include one or even several glass doors. The glass sits in a rabbet (rather than fitting into grooves like a wood panel), so it can be removed and replaced in case of damage. Once set into the rabbet, the glass may be attached with silicone sealant and perhaps glass points as well, or thin pieces of wood can be used to capture it. Another method is to rout a groove into which a specially made flexible panel retainer fits.

ANOTHER WAY TO INSTALL GLASS

Instead of routing a groove and inserting a retainer, as shown on p. 160, you could insert glazing points to hold the glass in place, then run a bead of latex or silicone caulk (which is stronger but will be more difficult to remove if you need to change the glass). Be sure the bead is not so wide as to make it visible from the other side.

1 Cut the rails and stiles to length and rout the cope cuts on the ends of the rails. Use a profile bit made for glass doors to cut the groove on the inside edges of all four pieces.

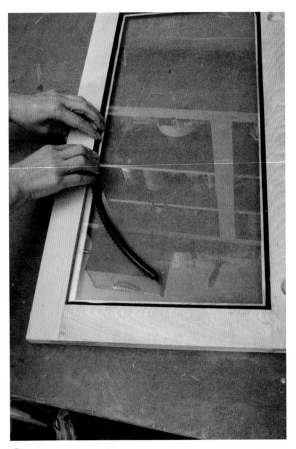

2 Install a groove-cutting router bit made to be used with the panel retainer (Step 3). Position the router so it cuts a groove that will be slightly behind the glass when it is installed. Cut the groove all along the length of the rails (top). For the stiles, do not cut the groove completely through the length or the groove will be visible when the door is assembled. Instead, start and end the groove cut 1 in. or so from the stiles' ends (bottom).

3 Cut pieces of panel retainer, with mitered corners at each end, with scissors. Press the retainer into place to secure the glass.

finishing and installing

YOU'VE SPENT so much time and effort building cabinet cases, drawer bodies, and doors that you may be tempted to treat applying finish, attaching the cabinets, and installing hardware as mere after-thoughts. But these elements go a long way toward defining the look and durability of your kitchen cabinets, so take the time to choose the best products and apply them with care.

Probably the most common order of work is to finish the cabinets and doors, add hardware, and then install the cabinets. However, don't hesitate to change this order if it suits your workflow. In particular, you may choose to add the hardware and install drawers last, after installing the cabinet cases.

A good finish dresses up a cabinet and makes it easy to wipe clean. Until fairly recently, it took special equipment, expensive materials, and a good deal of practiced skill to apply effective stains and paints. If you want to get real fancy with lacquer, shellac, or other traditional finishes, consult a book such as *Taunton's Complete Illustrated Guide to Finishing,* which discusses a variety of finish options. But fortunately, a good number of easy-to-apply finishes are available today, and this chapter emphasizes those.

Today's knobs, pulls, and drawer glides install easily and quickly, but beware: It's easy to make mistakes. Follow installation steps systematically, checking alignment as you go, so you end up with neatly positioned pulls and glides that operate smoothly. Also consider installing accessories and add-ons to improve convenience and make the most of your cabinet spaces.

Once cabinets are installed, countertops can be added. This is usually done by specialists, and I'll show you how they work. You may be able to do at least some of the work yourself.

Finishing

Kitchen cabinets generally are not finished with the same precision as fine furniture. In particular, the insides of cases are not expected to be perfect. But the doors, drawer faces, and front cabinet edges or frames are often viewed close up and should have a consistent appearance.

tip

You may choose to go with a rustic look, with knots and surface imperfections that lend character; a semicasual appearance, where a few minor imperfections and perhaps brush strokes are acceptable or even welcome; or a pristine and glassy-smooth surface, which has no flaws. Of course, the last option will require a good deal more work and skill than the others.

WHEN TO FINISH

The number one foe of a fine finish is dust, so the best time to finish is whenever you can apply finish in a dust-free environment. Unless you have a dedicated dustless finish room (and if you do, the rest of us envy you), the best option may be to wait until all the cabinets are built (or all the components are cut); then sand them smooth; then vacuum away all dust with a HEPA or other fine-filtered shop vacuum; then wait a day for even the tiniest dust motes to settle before you finish. While you work and for hours or even a day afterward (depending on the type of finish), take care not to introduce any dust into the room where you are finishing.

REPAIRING DENTS

Gouges and holes usually cannot be repaired, only filled, which is a good solution if you plan to paint. But surprisingly often, dents can be repaired in a way that makes the wood stainable. Dampen a rag, place it over the dent, and press a household iron set on high onto the rag. If that doesn't raise the dent, set the iron to steam and press it directly. More often than not, the dent will raise, and you can sand it smooth.

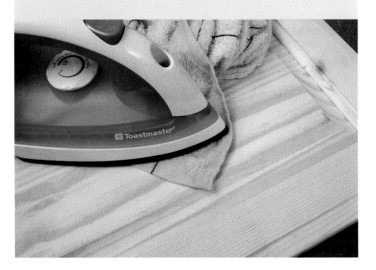

FRAME-AND-PANEL FINISHING

If your door is made with a frame and panel, remember that the panel will move—expand and contract—with changes in humidity, causing it to slightly change position in relation to the frame. Ideally, the panel and frames should be made and finished separately, allowed to dry, and then assembled; that will allow the panel to move inside the frame without resistance from the finish. In the real world, however, that is often not possible; it would cause a serious workflow problem when building a number of doors.

What to do? Many cabinetmakers shrug and say that things have a tendency to work out. Here are some possible solutions:

- Acrylic products—both paints and finishes—remain flexible. (An old dried acrylic paint chip will bend quite a bit before breaking.) This flexibility absorbs a good deal of panel movement.

- Some cabinetmakers apply a coat of finish to the panel—or just to the outside routed edges of the panel—ahead of time. After assembling the panel, they apply more finish, taking care to

tip Before you sand and apply finish, take the time to experiment. On large scrap pieces of plywood and hardwood of the same species as the cabinets, sand and apply all coats of the planned finish. That may mean, for example, primer and paint or stain and two coats of sealer. Don't skimp on the testing; for instance, a second coat of sealer can change the appearance significantly. Hold the test boards in several places in the kitchen and at different times of day, so you can see what the finish will look like in real-life conditions.

Sand all the flat areas on your cabinets with a random-orbit sander and then move on to other hand-sanding tools as needed for curved surfaces and tight corners.

apply it lightly to the joints between panel and frame. This allows the panel to move without cracking the finished surface.

- If you plan to wipe or brush the finish onto a finished door, take care not to fill the joint between panel and frame. Use your final stroke to wipe away any excess finish or paint in the joint.

PREPPING

To achieve professional results, you will probably spend a great deal more time preparing the wood than you will applying the finish.

If you will paint, fill all dents with wood putty or filler, allow to dry, and sand smooth. If you will stain and/or finish, minimize the filler as much as possible. Some fillers advertised as stainable will definitely not look like the surrounding wood surface once the finish is applied. You will probably get better results by staining first, then applying tinted wood filler; many colors are available. But don't expect the filled areas to be invisible; even if the color matches, the lack of grain lines will be noticeable.

Begin with a random-orbit sander to sand the flat areas. This tool often works for some gently curved areas as well but does not do a good job in

tip

Before sanding, consult your finish's label. Some finishes call for a very smooth surface, perhaps using 400-grit paper for the final sanding; others recommend a slightly rougher surface, perhaps finishing with 120-grit paper.

tight corners. The random-orbit sander will leave swirl marks even if you end up using 400-grit paper, so go over the area with a hand sander, stroking with the grain, before applying stain or finish.

You will likely use a variety of hand-sanding tools. A woodworking sanding block handles a variety of situations. A sanding sponge works well on many curved surfaces but not as well for sharp corners. It sometimes helps to use a small piece of sandpaper alone, perhaps folded over for tight spots or wrapped around a finger for curves. In a difficult situation, it may be worth the effort to make a custom sanding block: Cut a small piece of wood to match the contours of the area, and wrap sandpaper around it.

tip

Be kind to your lungs. Position fans to blow gently in and out of the room, to exchange the air without introducing dust. If you're using a product containing oil, lacquer, alcohol, or other toxic ingredients, wear a respirator. As a general rule, if you can strongly smell the finish, it's time to get a new respirator filter or introduce better ventilation. Even acrylic products can be harmful; ventilate the room and wear at least a dust mask.

After sanding, vacuum away all the dust you can using a fine-filtered shop vacuum or dust collector. Then wipe with a tack cloth or a lint-free cotton cloth (such as an old T-shirt) that has been laundered and is slightly dampened with turpentine, oil varnish, or a diluted version of the finish you will apply. As a final step, you can use your hand, which has natural oils.

FINISH OPTIONS

A dizzying array of wood finishes can be found at paint stores and home centers, and cabinetmakers offer a wide range of opinions on the best products. Here I emphasize the simplest ones to apply.

Staining. If you need to change the color of the wood, there are a good number of stains to choose among. An acrylic wiping stain is a good choice; it can be applied with a rag or brush without producing streaks. Dyes also work well and are recommended for difficult-to-stain woods, like pine and cherry. Gel stains, standard wood stains, and combination stain-and-finish products are not recommended; they can be streaky and difficult to control.

Spraying. Often spray finishes are applied with a HVLP sprayer, which produces a fine mist with minimal overspray, so it's easy to control. It usually has a hose that reaches into a can of finish. However, an HVLP requires a powerful compressor, which makes it expensive. An LVLP sprayer (see p. 35) produces similar results, though more slowly, and can be operated with a standard-size compressor. It typically has a small attached canister, which you need to refill fairly often.

To spray, place a door on a surface that can be rotated or position a cabinet case where you can easily reach all the parts to be coated. Turn on the compressor and briefly test-spray a nearby surface, to be sure the spray is not producing globules. Keep the sprayer moving as you work; stopping for even a half second may cause excessive buildup. Move the sprayer in one direction and release the trigger when you reach the end of a stroke; holding the trigger as you reverse direction will also produce buildup.

These acrylic stains are made for wiping or brushing on.

ROTISSERIE SPRAYING

A rotisserie painting caddy rotates easily, so you can quickly spray all edges of a door. You can make one simply by attaching a circular piece of plywood to a kitchen lazy susan. A grid of hold-ups can be made of most anything; in this case, the cabinetmaker used hold-offs designed for concrete forms, but something like 16d finish nails or 3-in. screws would also work.

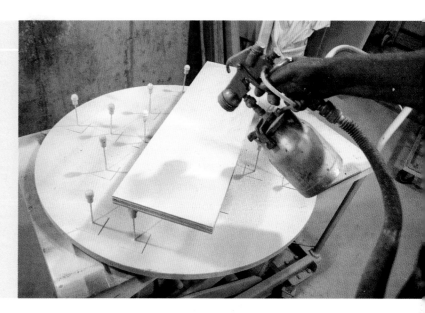

A nearby block wall is a fine place for testing a spray pattern before application. A sheet of dry-wall or some scrap plywood would also work.

Conversion varnish and nitrocellulose lacquer are often sprayed by professionals. Lacquer in particular calls for care and skill and requires multiple coats, so it may be too difficult for a beginner. Acrylic cabinet paint is another option: It is more forgiving, though you do need to be careful not to overspray.

Brushing and wiping. A number of good-looking and long-lasting products can be applied without a sprayer. These tend to be fairly thin and watery, allowing them to level out before drying, which eliminates wiping streaks or brush marks. You will probably need to apply two or more coats to achieve a hard-wearing surface. Some products call for light sanding between coats, while others need no sanding.

Wiping may sound tedious and time-consuming, but it is surprisingly easy and quick. Use a lint-free cotton cloth. In corners you will need to wipe against the grain, but try to finish using strokes that run with the grain. Fortunately, a bit of cross-grain wiping will not be visible.

For quicker application, you may find it easier to start by applying with an inexpensive foam brush, though standard brushes can work well. Apply liberally, then wipe with light strokes along the grain.

A drying rack holds plenty of doors while they dry, allowing you to keep working.

tips

Wood conditioner prevents a blotchy appearance and is a good idea for cherry, pine, some types of maple, and other touchy species. It is usually not needed for oak or birch.

Polyurethane finish is available in oil- and water-based versions. The oil-based option is more durable and scratch resistant but tends to yellow and it does not flex, which could cause problems with a frame-and-panel door (see pp. 162–163). Acrylic poly is pretty strong, but you may need to apply two or more coats. Most people prefer a satin finish, but high-gloss versions are also available.

Urethane acrylic and waterborne paints work well for cabinets. They spray or brush on easily and generally do not require priming first. Some types cannot be thinned with water; you must buy the company's proprietary thinner.

Here are three products that can be applied with a rag or with a brush followed by a rag.

Cabinet Hardware

Nearly all the hardware used on kitchen cabinets is of three types: drawer slides (also called glides), hinges, and pulls or knobs. None is difficult to install.

HINGES

Most hinges used today are concealed, or Euro-style. Not only are they easy to install but they can be quickly adjusted, so you can align your doors to achieve neat parallel lines between doors as well as between doors and other horizontal surfaces. These hinges also allow for doors to be adjusted up and down.

Euro-style hinges typically come in two parts, the hinge arm, which attaches to the door via a fairly large hole drilled partway through the door, and a plate that attaches to the cabinet. You will need a Forstner® bit to match the size of your hinge—usually 35mm, or $1\frac{3}{8}$ in.

Before boring holes in your cabinet doors, do a test run. Follow the steps on a scrap piece of plywood and make sure the cup hole is the correct depth, the hinge will overlay the cabinet the desired distance, and the door will open the distance you want.

Buying hinges. Hinge options may seem confusing, but in most cases this is what you will need:

- Get full overlay hinges.
- Choose a mounting plate for the amount you want to overlay the frame or case edge. The most common overlay is $\frac{1}{2}$ in.

tip

In this book, I install hardware, doors, and drawers first, then install the cabinets. However, you may choose to install the cabinet cases first.

tip

It's common to drill the holes for the hinges 3 in. or 4 in. from the top and bottom of the door, but this distance is not important. Just make sure the hinges will not interfere with a shelf or interior hardware.

- Most doors should open at 100° to 120°, which provides plenty of access to the inside of the cabinet. However, if a cabinet has pullout trays, the drawers need to open wider—165° is common. Angled corner cabinet doors need to open only at 45°, so 45° hinges are often used.

- Order all the hinges you need from an online source or a cabinet supplier. You'll need two hinges for most doors, but three or four hinges for tall pantry doors.

SELF-CENTERING DRILL BIT

Cabinet hardware should be attached with screws that are perfectly perpendicular to the wood, so their heads lie nice and flat. (Non-flat screw heads can mean that doors will not close all the way.) You may think you can do this freehand, but, actually, almost nobody can. A self-centering bit, often referred to by the brand name Vix®, drills a wonderfully straight pilot hole, making it easy to drive screws precisely. Buy self-centering bits for the size screws you will drive—most often, #3 or #5.

1 Drill holes in the doors. They must be a consistent distance from the door edge—typically, ¼ in. or ⅛ in. And the holes must be the correct depth. To achieve this, you can use a drill press with a fence that aligns the bit correctly. If you are drilling with a hand drill, make a simple jig, as shown, out of ¼-in. plywood and hold it against the edge of the door while you drill. The Forstner bit shown will have drilled to the correct depth when its top surface is flush with the wood surface.

tip

If you are unsure of your ability to drill a reasonably straight hole with a Forstner bit, you can purchase a drill jig that holds the bit straight and stops when you reach the correct depth. However, the shape of a Forstner bit makes it easy to drill holes that are at least close to straight vertical, and with a bit of practice you can learn to drill holes of the correct depth.

2 Insert the hinge's cup into the hole you just drilled, and use a square to hold the hinge square to the door. Drill pilot holes using a self-centering bit (top), then drive mounting screws (above). Attach both hinges.

4 Adjust the door up or down by loosening the plate screws, moving the door, and tightening the screws. Use the adjusting screws to move the top or bottom of the door in or out.

3 Attach the mounting plates to the hinges, open the hinges to 90°, and position the door where you want it to go. It helps to clamp a board at the bottom of the cabinet to support the door as you work. Hook the plates' small front tabs to the front of the door. To attach the mounting plates, drive screws through the centers of the slots so you can adjust the door up or down.

DRAWER SLIDES

Choose drawer slides (or glides) to suit the situation:

- Inexpensive slides with nylon rollers are fine for small drawers that do not hold much weight. They are easy to install and are forgiving of minor imperfections in the cabinet or drawer body. However, they take up ½ in. of space on each side, so the drawer box needs to be 1 in. narrower than the opening. And they allow you to pull the drawers out only about three-quarters of the way.

- For heavier-duty slides with guaranteed smooth operation under pressure, choose ball-bearing side-mounted slides. They also are ½ in. thick, so the drawer body must be 1 in. narrower than the opening. Less-expensive slides allow you to pull the drawer out most of the way.

- Full-extension slides work as advertised, and permit the drawer to be pulled out all the way, for easy access to items in the back.

- Self-closing and soft-closing slides gently complete the closing action in slow motion.

- Undermount slides attach to the bottom of the drawer, so you can build a box that is nearly as wide as the opening. However, these are expensive and difficult to install.

Installing nylon-roller slides. These come in two parts for each side. Look for lettering that tells you where each part goes: *CR* means cabinet right; *DL* means drawer left.

1 Line up the D parts (called glides) of the slide with the front (nonroller) edge nearly flush with the front edge of the drawer. Drill self-centering pilot holes (p. 168) and drive the provided screws.

2 Attach the C parts (called runners) to the cabinet. The front edge (which has a roller) should be about ⅛ in. back from the cabinet's edge. Use a framing square to align the runner so it is square to the cabinet's front edge. Drill self-centering pilot holes and drive screws to attach.

ATTACHING RUNNERS TO A FACE FRAME CABINET

If the cabinet has a face frame, you'll need to add wood to the inside side of the cabinet (as shown) to keep the runner parallel. Attach strips of wood the same thickness as the inside lip of the face frame (you may need to rip-cut them) to the cabinet before attaching the runners.

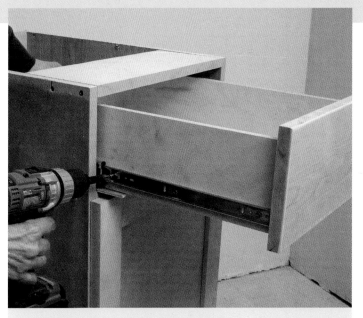

3 Test that the drawer operates smoothly; both drawer rollers should rest firmly on the runners all along their length. Push down on each front corner. If the drawer bounces up and down, you need to lower the runner on that side.

A ¼-in. piece of plywood works well as a spacer when installing drawer faces.

INSTALLING ROLLER SLIDES

Manufacturers make a variety of slide types, and you should check their installation instructions before installing. Here's one common method: Open the slides, and attach the portions that stay in the cabinet. Make sure the slides are square to the front of the cabinet. Use spacers if you have a face frame, as shown on the facing page. Set the drawer body on ¼-in. spacers at the bottom, so the drawer is centered in the opening. Push the drawer most of the way into the opening. Pull the slides out and attach the slides to the drawer with screws. Pull the drawer out farther and attach more screws.

ATTACHING DRAWER FACES

Once the drawer bodies are installed and can glide smoothly, the drawer faces are easy to install, usually with four screws driven through the inside of the drawer body, so no fasteners are visible on the face. However, take care to align the faces so they are parallel with doors and other drawers, and so that gaps between them are consistent.

If a door or a lower drawer face is already installed, check that it is straight, then simply use a spacer to hold the new drawer face parallel to it and at the desired height. In other situations, you may need to clamp boards to the cabinet to act as guides.

tip

The installation screws that come with your knobs or pulls may not be the right length, so you might need to buy longer ones. They are usually 8–32 machine screws with fine threads, but take a sample knob with you to the store, to make sure the new screws will fit.

PULLS AND KNOBS

Pulls and knobs are also simple to install: Drill holes of the correct size in the correct locations and attach with the screws provided. Knobs need only one screw, while pulls call for two.

Knobs and pulls are usually installed on the center of a drawer face, though with a wide face you may want to raise it up to the top third. On doors, they are often installed on the stile opposite the hinge, centered about 4 in. from the top for base cabinets and 4 in. from the bottom on wall cabinets. But this is not a rule, and you may choose other locations.

Most knobs and pulls provide very little leeway for covering drilling mistakes. Once you've drilled a mounting hole you can't undrill it, so work carefully to get the holes just right. Don't measure for each hole with a tape measure or square; the chance of error is too great. Instead, buy or make a reliable jig that's easy to hold in place and drill through.

A homemade jig like this can be flipped over, to align for holes on either side of a door. This one is made with pieces of ¼-in. plywood that are glued in place, but you can use most any material. Make sure the thin alignment strips on each side of the board are the same width and are all flush with the outside edge of the jig, so the measurements will be the same on each side. To use the jig, just place it on the door and drill through the holes.

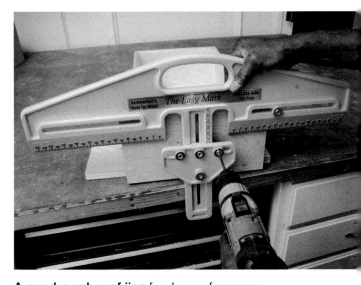

A good number of jigs for drawer faces are available for purchase. This one, by Sommerfeld, is bulky but easy to operate. Using various stops, center the jig on the drawer vertically and horizontally. If you will be installing knobs, just drill through the center hole. For pulls, use the two stops with holes, as shown.

Installing Cabinets

If kitchen walls are plumb and the floor is level, installing cabinets can usually proceed calmly and quickly. But surfaces are usually less than perfect, so you may need to spend a good deal of time shimming and filling in.

WORKING WITH OTHER TRADES

Kitchen remodeling usually involves running new electrical lines for receptacles and lights, and often also includes new piping for supply and drain lines. There may also be heating and air-conditioning ductwork to contend with. Whether the utilities have been hired out or you are installing them yourself, it's almost always best to have all the rough-in work done before installing cabinets.

Draw lines on the wall indicating where the cabinets will go, and check that everything will fit. Some particulars:

- Check that above-counter receptacles will be at the right height—at least 1 in. above the countertop backsplash, if there will be one.

- If the wall between the countertop and the bottom of wall cabinets will be tiled or otherwise covered, this should probably be done after the cabinets are installed, but check with the tiler to be sure.

tip

Resist the temptation to follow an out-of plumb or nonlevel wall or floor when installing cabinets. It may sound easier, but in the end it usually creates difficult problems. Shim as needed to make cabinets perfectly level and plumb.

- Make sure that cables or cords for under-cabinet lighting are installed at the correct height—often, just below the bottom of the cabinet.

- The dishwasher should be installed, or the lines—for electrical, drain, and water supply—should be in place or at least planned.

- Be very clear as to the required openings for appliances: dishwasher, refrigerator, and range or cooktop. Make sure the wiring and plumbing lines are in place.

- It's usually best to install new flooring before installing cabinets. If the flooring will be added later, you may need to raise the base cabinets (and the wall cabinets as well) to accommodate the extra floor height.

This cabinet had to be notched to accommodate the cable for a receptacle. In most cases, cables are run inside walls.

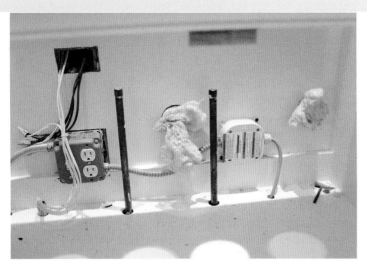

Under a sink, holes may need to be drilled and rectangles cut out of the back of a cabinet to accommodate plumbing and electrical lines. To accomplish this, you may need to coordinate with the plumber and electrician.

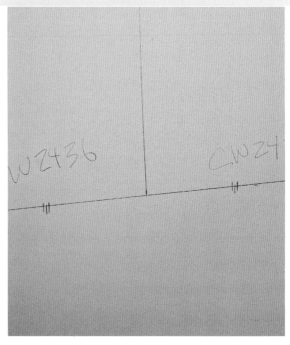

Mark the walls for the locations of the cabinets. Use a stud finder or drill exploratory holes to locate studs.

PREPPING

Check all the walls and floors for plumb and square. If the wall behind base cabinets is out of plumb or the floor is not level, you may need to shim cabinets at the floor or the wall, which may affect the final height of the cabinets.

WALL CABINETS

It's usually easier to install wall cabinets before base cabinets. Double-check the height—usually 18 in. above the top of the countertop or 54 in. above the floor. Make a couple of T-shaped braces, $1/2$ in. or so taller than the height of the cabinet underside. Position them at an angle to the wall, so you can adjust their height, and use them to temporarily hold the cabinets.

Wall cabinets must be attached to wall studs with screws driven through structural parts of the cabinet. So don't drive screws only through a $1/4$-in. plywood back; drive through $3/4$-in. plywood or through top and bottom cleats.

If there is a corner wall cabinet, start there. Work with a helper to get both sides and both faces

Once the first cabinet is installed plumb in both directions, clamp succeeding cabinets together, drill pilot holes through the frame (if any), and drive screws to attach.

> If the back wall is wavy, play it safe and install the first cabinets—often in the corner—slightly shimmed out from the wall. That will compensate for outward protrusions of the wall when installing the other cabinets.

plumb—you may need to use shims—and install with screws driven into studs.

To install adjoining cabinets, temporarily support them from below, and firmly clamp cabinets together, taking care to get the front faces and the tops and bottoms flush. Check for plumb, and install shims as needed. If the cabinets have face frames, drill pilot holes and drive cabinet screws

through the face frames to hold the cabinets together. For frameless cabinets, pilot holes are usually not needed. If you don't like the look of screw heads, countersink standard headed screws, then plug and sand the holes.

BASE CABINETS

To install base cabinets, adjust the legs or shim the kick plate frame (pp. 108–109) until they are at the correct height, are level with each other, and are plumb in the front.

Openings for the dishwasher, refrigerator, range, and other appliances need to be precisely correct at the top, bottom, and sides; getting this right might call for painstaking shimming.

Attach the base cabinets to the walls with screws driven into studs. Because base cabinets rest on the floor, these screws do not have to be very strong but they should hold firmly.

You may choose to cover the kick plate with a trim piece of wood or with vinyl cove base.

CABINET SCREWS

Many cabinets are installed with drywall or all-purpose screws, which usually work just fine. But they can sometimes break; their heads strip out easily, making them difficult to remove if you need to reposition a cabinet; and they're kind of ugly. Instead, spend a bit more money for cabinet screws, which have attractive heads, are sure to stay strong, have self-tapping threads to make them easier to drive, and have star-shaped drives that are much less likely to strip out.

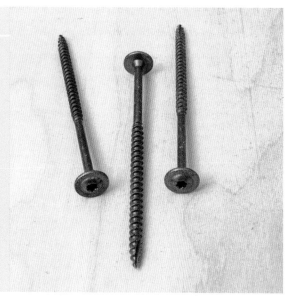

You'll probably need to add small trim or fill-in pieces to make up the gaps between cabinets and walls or, in this case, a farmhouse sink.

At the dishwasher opening, the cabinets need to be perfectly spaced and perfectly parallel, for a professional appearance. (This dishwasher allows for installing a decorative face on the drawer, and a face matching the cabinetry was installed.)

Amenities

Cabinets can be outfitted with a variety of accessories that help make the best use of space and provide easy access to their contents. Here are some tips on installing them. The units here, which are all from Rev-A-Shelf, come with sliding and attachment hardware and can be purchased to fit most any size opening.

A bit of visual interest is supplied at this end panel by adding what is essentially a cabinet door to one section, and trimming out the other section.

A wood drawer organizer can be cut to fit the drawer as needed. It does not need to be as wide as the drawer because space on one or both sides can serve as an additional storage pocket. Once the basic organizer is in place, no more cutting is needed: Three sizes of spacers further subdivide this drawer, slipping into place via a series of mounting holes.

A slide-out shelf may attach to the sides of the cabinets, using standard drawer hardware. Or, as shown here, it may have bottom-mounted hardware. Installation is simple: Attach the sliding unit with screws to the floor of the cabinet, keeping the front tabs parallel to the cabinet's front. Then slide the drawer in.

Slide-out units can house one or more garbage receptacles. They hide unattractive trash, yet make for easy access. This sliding unit attaches to the bottom of the cabinet much like the slide-out shelf above. The unit could be installed so you open the door and then pull it out, but attaching the drawer to the front makes it easier to use. Slide the unit out slightly and mark where the door should attach; this may take a bit of trial and error. Attach the back of the door to the unit's mounting plate with two short screws. Slide the door back

into place and check alignment; you may or may not need to remove screws in order to make the adjustments. The unit slides smoothly enough that the door pull can be at the side, as shown, or you may choose to move the pull to the center top of the door.

This shelf unit makes good use of a blind base cabinet corner. Two shelves, attached to a vertical pole mounted just inside the cabinet door, swing out to provide easy access to a kitchen's darkest recessed space.

This lazy susan has expandable center poles, so you can adjust shelf height. Use the template provided to drill pilot holes in the centers of the top and bottom of the cabinet, then install the parts—the roller units, the pole, flanges, shelves, and a mounting plate at the top. The upper shelf can then be adjusted for height.

Countertops

Countertops are installed after the cabinets are in place. They usually overhang the cabinets by 1 in. to 2 in. in front and on the sides. Most are structurally strong enough so that support is needed only every 24 in. or more. Thus you probably do not need to provide support where the top spans a dishwasher. Your cabinets should be nice and level, but it's the countertop company's job to shim the top so it is perfectly level in both directions.

A concrete countertop that is only lightly tinted retains some of its natural gray color and harmonizes well with the blue-gray cabinetry.

AVAILABLE MATERIALS

Granite and quartz are the most popular materials these days, but you may want to consider other options. Some types can be installed by a do-it-yourselfer, but most benefit from professional installation.

Concrete. Once a daring choice, concrete countertops have gone mainstream. Concrete tops require a regular application of sealer to prevent staining. They may be nearly uniform in color or can have splashes of various hues and even incorporate artistic touches, like glass or pebble aggregates or hand-painted tints made to imitate granite veining. An expert installer can give you a predictable result or create a work of art. If you want to try your hand at making a concrete top yourself, there are a number of websites that sell kits and give step-by-step directions. Concrete tops weigh somewhat

THE SINK

A self-rimming sink, which sits on top of the countertop, is the easiest and least-expensive sink option, but some people find the elevated rim annoying to wipe around. If you want to make it easy to wipe crumbs right into the sink, install an undermount sink. In that case, the perimeter edges of the countertop will be exposed, so these countertops are traditionally made of polished granite, concrete, or quartz. Farmhouse sinks, which are large and are sometimes called apron sinks because of their wide exposed fronts, are also popular and are usually undermounted as well.

Farmhouse sink with countertop at the same level as the sink.

Farmhouse sink with countertop that rests on top.

Self-rimming sink.

A speckled granite countertop that is only ¾ in. thick exhibits class without calling attention to itself.

Quartz countertop patterns run the gamut from one solid color to strikingly bold patterns. This elegant example falls right in the middle.

Laminates are not only inexpensive but can also be great looking. They can mimic the look of other materials, such as stone, but also are available in solid colors and unique patterns.

more than other countertops, but as long as the top is not excessively thick it can be supported by traditional cabinetry.

Granite. Granite may be light or dark, speckled, or with pronounced grain. Edges can be squared off, rounded, or ogee shaped. Because granite is a natural stone, granite tops have one-of-a-kind patterns that range from subtle to striking. Sealer should be applied a couple of times per year, especially with lighter colors.

Quartz. Quartz countertops are constructed from a manmade product composed of over 90% quartz particles with resins and tints; it comes in completely predictable patterns. Quartz is actually more durable and stain resistant than granite.

Laminate. Sometimes called by the brand name Formica®, laminates are the least-expensive option. Today's laminates come in a wide variety of colors and patterns to coordinate with most any decor. Patterns that mimic natural stone are popular. Edges come in a variety of shapes. Laminates are surprisingly durable: They do not need to be sealed and can last for many decades.

Tile. Countertop tiles (do not use wall tiles, which will crack) come in just about any color you can imagine. Glazed tiles themselves are impervious to staining, but the grout lines need to be kept well sealed. Granite tiles can be installed with very thin grout lines, or even with no grout lines at all.

Solid-surface. Often referred to by the brand name Corian®, older solid-surface countertops tended to get dull after years of wiping, but today's materials are harder and retain a shiny surface. They also come in a dizzying array of colors and patterns. Often a sink is molded into the top seamlessly, which makes cleaning easy. These materials can be installed only by factory-licensed pros.

Ceramic tiles with a stone look and wide grout lines create an informal look. With yearly applications of sealers, the surface is easy to clean.

This bright solid-surface countertop has an integral sink that makes cleaning a breeze.

INSTALLING GRANITE AND QUARTZ COUNTERTOPS

Granite and quartz (and sometimes marble, though most marbles are easily scratched and stained) countertops are almost always cut, shaped, and smoothed in a special shop. However, after the initial large cut, most of the work could be accomplished by a skilled DIYer with a common 4-in. or 5-in. grinder, plus about $250 worth of blades and polishing wheels.

It is possible to buy granite slabs from online sources or from some tile stores or stone yards. They may come with one smoothed edge. Cut your granite with a circular saw or grinder and a good diamond blade and have a helper drizzle water onto the blade with a hose as you cut. With a belt sander you can generally smooth the cut edge but not make it shiny. To take it to the next level and create edges that are smooth and shiny, you'll need an abrasive wheel and a set of stone polishing wheels.

1 At a stone shop, large rough-edged slabs are cut using a massive diamond-cutting saw.

2 To make a cutout for an undermounted sink (where the cut edges of the granite will be exposed), workers draw the outline using a Wite-Out® pen from a stationary store. They cut roughly with a grinder equipped with a diamond blade.

3 At tight corners, the grinder is used to make a series of short cuts up to the cut line. Then the diamond blade is used as a scraper to produce a rounded edge.

4 An abrasive wheel (being used on a marble top with no water here) defines the curved line.

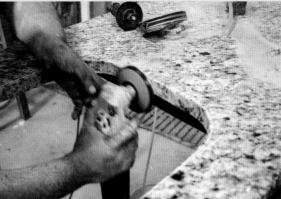

5 Once the line has been cut and generally smoothed, a series of abrasive pads are used to polish the edge. Start with a 200-grit pad, and then polish with pads of 400 grit, 800 grit, and 1,500 grit. If you want it super smooth, finish with a 3,000-grit wheel.

6 Work done at the shop is not always perfect, but a good deal of cutting and polishing can be performed in the field. Here, a slab had to be rip-cut and have its edge polished. Using pro-level blades and pads, the work can be done without water.

7 During installation, joints can be sealed with clear silicone, but pros mix a two-part epoxy with colorant to match the countertop (left). Installation must be done carefully, so all the edges line up perfectly; sealing around the sink is especially tricky (middle). A special electric tool (right) pulls two pieces very tightly together while the epoxy sets.

10 bathroom vanities

A STANDARD inexpensive bathroom vanity has a sink on top and two doors below. Inside, there is just one large open space. This arrangement makes for easy installation because it leaves plenty of room for the plumbing—the drain trap, the stop valves for hot and cold water, and the supply tubes running up to the faucet. However, when it comes to usable storage and convenience, there is much to be desired: You often have to get on your knees

to reach cleaning products, and there's plenty of wasted space.

The standard vanity is a good example of the disadvantages of one-size-fits-all cabinetry: Manufacturers do not know where your pipes are, so they just leave a large cavity. You, however, do know where your pipes are. And armed with the skills and tools shown throughout this book, you can plan and build a cabinet that will maximize your storage opportunities.

In this chapter I've featured two vanity projects. One project employs drawers and the other open shelving, but both can be modified to fit like a glove in your bathroom.

Choosing a Style

A vanity is a cabinet that houses a sink. (The other sink options—pedestal and wall hung—can be good looking but do not give you a place to store stuff.) The vanity's sink may be a separate unit that is mounted on a small countertop sometimes called a deck. Or, as seen in the two projects in this chapter, it can be integral with the countertop. This option has the advantages of a seamless look, easy cleaning, and no worries about caulking the sink to the top. Style possibilities for bathroom counters are as varied as kitchen counters.

This floating vanity hovers above the floor, making for easy cleaning. A wide vanity like this may be made as one large unit, or it may be made up of two or three units fastened together during installation.

A bowl sink makes a dramatic and lively design statement. It may be mounted onto a wood deck that is well protected with paint. A better arrangement is to fasten it to a waterproof surface like the countertop top shown here.

Planning Your Bathroom Layout

If you are remodeling a bathroom, carefully plan the size and placement of all the elements—bathtub, toilet, vanity with sink, and any other storage or plumbing features. Consult a contractor or a building inspector to be sure you follow local building codes. Common codes, as well as lessons learned by designers over the years, have led to guidelines (which may also be laws) illustrated in "Sink and Vanity Dimensions" on p. 186.

- A GFCI receptacle should be within 3 ft. of the sink. There are no clear guidelines on how close it can be, but it should be located where it cannot get splashed with water.

- There should be at least 8 in. between the vanity cabinet and a tub, to allow for the shower

A console sink is a simple structure that provides a vintage look. It leaves the plumbing on display, so plan to replace plastic or old plumbing with gleaming chrome or stainless-steel parts. You may add a shelf, if desired.

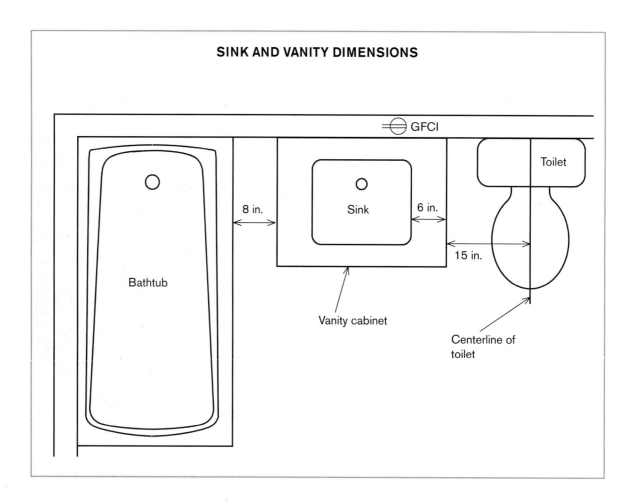

SINK AND VANITY DIMENSIONS

GFCI

Toilet

Bathtub

8 in.

Sink

6 in.

15 in.

Vanity cabinet

Centerline of toilet

---

curtain to be easily drawn and to keep the vanity from getting too wet.

- The distance from the vanity cabinet to the center of the toilet should be at least 15 in.; any closer will feel overly cozy.

- On each side of the sink's bowl there should be at least 6 in. of counter (or deck) space, to keep water from splashing on the floor and to leave room for toothbrush and soap holders or dispensers and other toiletry objects. If you use an integral sink, this will be built in.

Vanity with Drawers

For storing cosmetics, soaps, toothpaste, and other bathroom items, nothing beats drawers. This unit squeezes in as much drawer space as possible.

The design is easily modified to fit your bathroom. This example uses a 31-in.-wide vanity sink top, but you could include a wider or narrower top as suits. The drawers are shown on the right here, but they could go on the left if the location of your plumbing so dictates. And if you enlarge the vanity, the drawers could be wider or you could go with a set of drawers on each side.

If the plumbing is smack dab in the middle of the vanity location, you may be able to move some or all of the plumbing over a bit, to allow you to enlarge the drawers. Cut out a section of drywall, shut off the water supply, and consult *Plumbing Complete* (Taunton Press, 2009) for instructions on cutting and attaching supply and drain lines.

VANITY WITH DRAWERS

In this design, the position of the vertical cabinet divider, which determines the width of the drawers, depends on the plumbing. All parts are ¾-in. plywood.

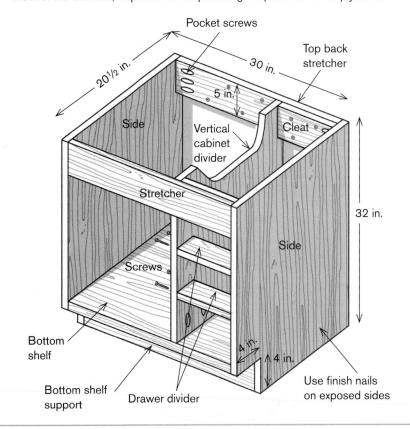

Pocket screws

Top back stretcher

20½ in.

30 in.

5 in.

Side

Vertical cabinet divider

Cleat

32 in.

Stretcher

Side

Screws

Bottom shelf

Bottom shelf support

Drawer divider

4 in.

4 in.

Use finish nails on exposed sides

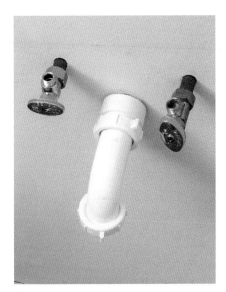

1 Using the guidelines on the facing page, determine the location and size of the vanity. The plumbing trap and supply lines need to go in the open cavity; unless you do some very fancy cutting or install shallow drawers, the plumbing cannot go behind the drawers (see Step 9 on p. 190).

2 Measure the integral sink and plan on a vanity that is about 1 in. narrower and shallower, so the sink will overhang ½ in. on the sides and 1 in. on the front. Also roughly measure the depth of the bowl; this will determine how high your top drawer can be.

3 Following "Vanity with Drawers" on p. 187, cut the side pieces, which have a cutout for a toekick. Also cut a stretcher for the top back, about 5 in. wide and the desired width of the vanity minus 1½ in. (28½ in. in this example). Cut two bottom shelf supports to the same length as the top back stretcher and 4 in. wide (the height of the toekick). Finally, cut a top front stretcher to the same length as the others and the width of the sink depth (Step 2).

4 Adhere edge-banding to the front edges of the sides (see pp. 57–58), which will be visible when the vanity is complete.

5 Attach the stretchers and bottom shelf supports to the sides of the vanity using pocket screws so no fasteners will be visible on the vanity sides (see pp. 64–65). Drill pocket-screw holes on the back sides of both ends of all four stretcher and support pieces. Drive 1¼-in. coarse-thread screws to attach to one side of the vanity, then tip the assembly up onto the other side and drive screws to attach to the other side of the vanity. Keep all surfaces flush as you attach them.

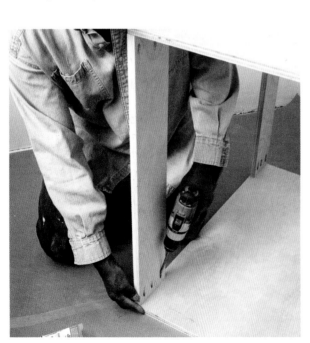

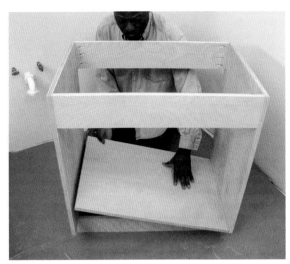

6 Cut a bottom shelf to the same width as the sides and the same length as the stretchers. (Measure the open space to be sure of the length.) Apply edge-banding to the front edge of the bottom shelf. Press it into place and attach the shelf to the bottom shelf supports with finish nails.

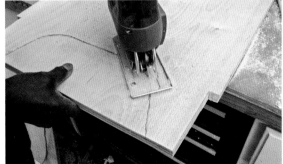

7 Cut a vertical cabinet divider which, along with a side piece, will complete the opening for the drawers. Make it the height from the bottom shelf to the top of the stretchers and the same width as the sides. Place the divider in the cabinet and mark it at the bottom of the stretcher, as shown, for notches on each side. Cut the notches and apply edge-banding to the front edge, which will be visible.

8 Mark for a cut out in the middle of the vertical cabinet divider that roughly follows the contours of the sink's underside. This does not need to be very accurate because it will not show. The bottom of the cutout should be the same dimension as the front stretcher (which was figured in Step 2), plus an inch or so. Draw freehand or use paint cans to mark for the curves. Cut with a jigsaw.

9 To determine the position of the vertical cabinet divider, place the sink in place on the vanity. Measure with a framing square and tape measure or put the divider in place and move it over as far as possible without interfering with the sink's plumbing. Check that it is square to the bottom shelf and to the top stretchers and mark its location at the bottom shelf and the top stretchers.

tip

When positioning the vertical cabinet divider, place the faucet in its holes and also check that the piece will not get in the way when you install the drain line to the trap.

10 To attach the vertical cabinet divider, cut two cleats about 4 in. wide, for the front and back stretchers, and attach them to the stretchers with 1¼-in. screws. Drive screws to attach the vertical cabinet divider to the cleats, as shown.

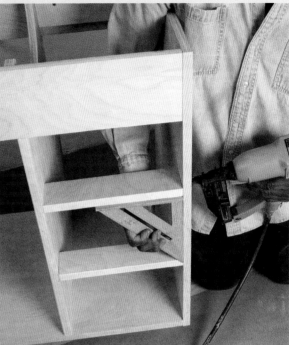

11 Confirm that the vertical cabinet divider is square to the bottom shelf and measure for the drawer dividers. Cut dividers that are 3 in. wide or so and apply edge-banding to the front edges. Mark the positions for the drawer dividers so the resulting openings will be ½ in. taller than the drawer boxes. Attach by applying glue and driving finish nails. (Use pocket screws if possible, but there will probably not be enough room to drive the screws.) As you work, check for square and see that the openings are consistent in dimensions.

12 Build drawer bodies that are 1 in. narrower and ½ in. shorter in height than the openings (see pp. 121–130). In most cases, 18-in.-deep drawers will work well. Build and attach a door with hinges, install the drawer hardware, and attach the pulls.

13 Move the cabinet into position. Set the sink top in place against the wall, and attach the plumbing trap and the supply lines to the faucet. Once the plumbing is installed, run a bead of adhesive caulk along the underside of the top to adhere it to the vanity.

Floating Vanity

A vanity that hangs from the wall with no legs or other visible means of support makes for easy cleaning and provides a fanciful, contemporary look. The project shown here has open shelving to accommodate storage baskets, but you could add doors or drawers.

A floating vanity must be very strong and must be securely attached to wall studs. The design shown here, which relies on interlocking dadoes for rigidity, has been built many times by Mike Fish of Vogon Construction in Chicago. He has personally stood and jumped on top of each one to test for strength. (He does this prior to installing the sink, of course.)

As with the vanity with drawers project, this design can be modified to fit neatly around your plumbing, for maximum storage space. In my example, the middle shelf (which isn't shown in the drawing) had to be cut only to accommodate the trap pipe that rises up to the sink. In your situation, you might need to cut around supply pipes as well.

This vanity is sized for a 31-in.-wide sink top but can be easily modified to suit other sizes. You may choose to install a wider vanity, with added countertop space. Also this vanity is 24 in. tall and is installed 8 in. above the floor, but depending on your vanity height preference you might choose to install it at a different height. You may also want a shorter unit, to make space for a wastebasket or storage section underneath.

FLOATING VANITY

Dadoes in the sides and the top make for an interlocking structure that is surprisingly strong, enabling this vanity to stay together, even when an adult leans or sits on it. The bottom, sides, and back are $\frac{3}{4}$-in. plywood. The middle shelf, which is not shown, is 29 in. by 21 in.

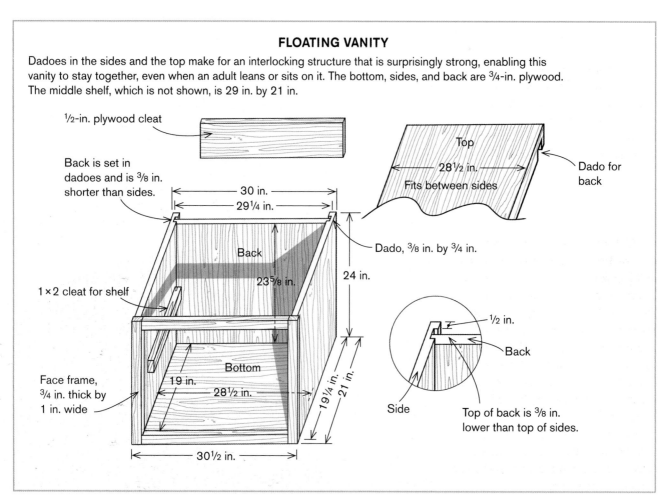

1/2-in. plywood cleat

Back is set in dadoes and is 3/8 in. shorter than sides.

Top

28 1/2 in.

Fits between sides

Dado for back

30 in.

29 1/4 in.

Dado, 3/8 in. by 3/4 in.

Back

23 5/8 in.

24 in.

1 × 2 cleat for shelf

1/2 in.

Back

Face frame, 3/4 in. thick by 1 in. wide

19 in.

Bottom

28 1/2 in.

19 1/4 in.

21 in.

Side

Top of back is 3/8 in. lower than top of sides.

30 1/2 in.

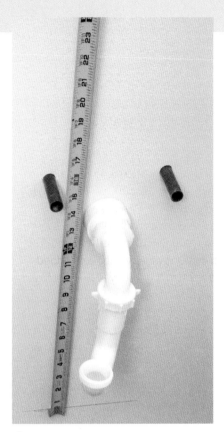

tips

If you are able to get to the wall framing, go ahead and install 2×10 blocking pieces that span stud to stud, then cover with drywall; that will give you extra fastening surface. But the added blocking is not required; attaching solidly to two wall studs (Step 9 on p. 196) will be plenty strong.

The photos in these steps show plywood that has been stained ahead of time. For maximum strength, make sure the wood remains unstained at the critical glue points—in the dadoes and at the ends of the back piece—because wood glue is strongest when applied to bare wood.

1 Measure your plumbing and plan for a vanity that makes good use of your space. You may find that moving the vanity up or down or to the side by a couple of inches can increase the usable space.

2 Cut the sides to length so they are 1¼ in. shorter than the depth of the sink top. (Once the face frame is added, the sink top will overhang the front of the vanity by ½ in.) Cut the back piece to a length 1¾ in. shorter than the length of the sink top. (Accounting for the thicknesses of the sides with dadoes, the sink top will overhang the vanity by ½ in. on each side.) The back should be ⅜ in. shorter than the sides, as shown, so that the top, which will also have a dado, can set into the back and come flush with the sides.

3 Set up a tablesaw or router table to cut a dado in the sides that is ¾ in. wide and ⅜ in. deep. Test the dado cut on a scrap piece, as shown.

tip

For an extra-tight fit, cut a dado that is precisely as wide as your plywood, typically, ²³/₃₂ in.

4 Cut the dadoes along the inside back edges of the side pieces. Slide the back piece into the dadoes you just cut in the side pieces and check that the back is ⅜ in. shorter than the sides. Attach the sides to the back by applying glue and driving finishing nails. Reinforce the joint by driving 2-in. wood or deck screws every 6 in. or so. (Do not use drywall or all-purpose screws, which are not very strong.)

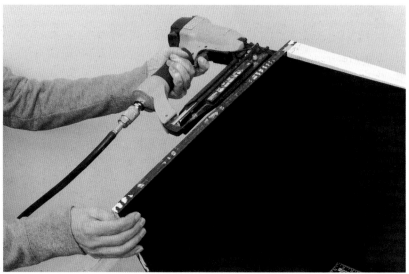

5 Measure and cut the bottom piece to fit. Attach with glue and finish nails. Reinforce with screws.

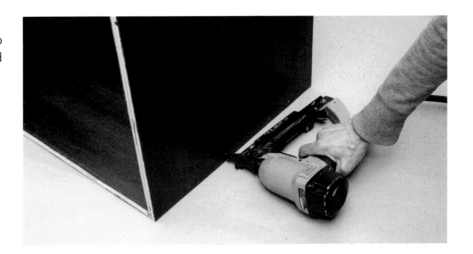

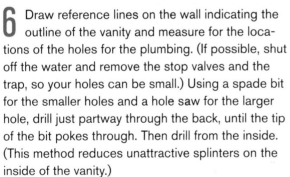

6 Draw reference lines on the wall indicating the outline of the vanity and measure for the locations of the holes for the plumbing. (If possible, shut off the water and remove the stop valves and the trap, so your holes can be small.) Using a spade bit for the smaller holes and a hole saw for the larger hole, drill just partway through the back, until the tip of the bit pokes through. Then drill from the inside. (This method reduces unattractive splinters on the inside of the vanity.)

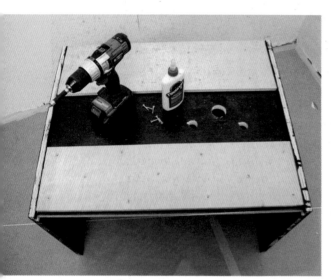

7 Add ½-in. plywood cleats to the back at the top and the bottom. Keep the top cleat ⅜ in. below the top of the back piece. Drive a grid of 1-in. screws to fasten the cleats securely.

8 Measure and cut the top piece to fit between the sides. Using the same dado setup as in Step 3 (p. 194), cut a dado in the underside of the top at the back. The top piece should fit snugly via its dado onto the back piece and come flush with the top of the side pieces. Attach with glue and nails and reinforce with screws.

9 Line up the holes you cut in the back piece with your plumbing. Use temporary supports to hold the vanity in place and check for plumb. Locate the wall studs and start driving 3-in. cabinet screws (not drywall or all-purpose screws) through the back and into the studs.

tip

Locate the studs precisely, so you drive screws into their centers for maximum strength.

10 Drive 2-in. deck or wood screws through the top and anywhere else that might need reinforcement. Sit or stand on the vanity, to make sure it is solid and unmovable.

11 Cut holes for the sink top's bowl and the faucet. Measure carefully (or use a template, if provided), so you cut only as much as you need to. Even with a large cutout, the top will still be plenty strong.

12 Attach the necessary plumbing, in this case stop valves and the trap. Cut a middle shelf to fit and cut notches as needed to accommodate the plumbing. Attach cleats to the inside of the sides for the shelf to rest on. (Don't attach the middle shelf because you may need to repair the plumbing in the future.)

13 Cut and attach 1× face-frame pieces that are 1 in. wide. Set the sink top in place and attach the faucet, supply lines, and the drain trap. Run a bead of adhesive caulk under the sink to secure it to the vanity.

credits

index